9604 ✳

Cambridge Proficiency
Examination Practice 6

Cambridge Proficiency

Examination Practice 6

University of Cambridge
Local Examinations Syndicate

CAMBRIDGE
UNIVERSITY PRESS

PUBLISHED BY THE PRESS SYNDICATE OF THE UNIVERSITY OF CAMBRIDGE
The Pitt Building, Trumpington Street, Cambridge CB2 1RP, United Kingdom

CAMBRIDGE UNIVERSITY PRESS
The Edinburgh Building, Cambridge, CB2 2RU, United Kingdom
40 West 20th Street, New York, NY 10011-4211, USA
10 Stamford Road, Oakleigh, Melbourne 3166, Australia

First published 1996
Third printing 1998

Printed in the United Kingdom at the University Press, Cambridge

ISBN 0 521 56663 0 Student's Book
ISBN 0 521 56662 2 Teacher's Book
ISBN 0 521 56661 4 Set of 2 cassettes

Contents

Acknowledgements

The publishers are grateful to the following for permission to reproduce copyright material. It has not always been possible to identify sources of all the material used, and in such cases the publishers would welcome information from the copyright owners.

Texts: Thames & Hudson for the extract on pp. 48–9 from *Writing: the story of alphabets and scripts* by Georges Jean © 1992; the extract on pp. 50–51 from *Paul Scott – A life* by Hilary Spurling, Hutchinson, © 1990, is reprinted by permission of David Higham Associates; the extract on pp. 59–60 from *Escape Attempts* by Stanley Cohen and Laurie Taylor, Penguin, © 1976, is reprinted by permission of the Peters Fraser & Dunlop Group Ltd; the extract on pp. 73–4 from *The Killjoy* by Anne Fine, originally published by Bantam Black Swan, 1986, now published by Penguin Books (UK) and Warner Books (USA) is reproduced by permission of Murray Pollinger; Penguin Books for the extract on pp. 75–6 from *Selected Essays and Articles* by John Berger, © John Berger 1972; Triad Grafton for the extract on p. 96 from *Look at Me* by Anita Brookner, © Anita Brookner 1985.

Photographs by Art Directors/Yoav Levy/Phototake NYC on page 129 (below centre); Associated Press/Topham Picturepoint on page 129 (above left); Barnaby's Picture Library on page 123 (above); Cambridgeshire Fire and Rescue Service on page 117 (below); Camera Press Limited on page 119; The J. Allan Cash Photolibrary on pages 118, 124; Sally and Richard Greenhill on page 115; Robert Harding Picture Library on page 129 (below right); Gamma/Alexis Duclos/ICRC on page 117 (above), Steinemann/ICRC on page 114 (above); The Image Bank/Alvis Upitis on page 123 (below), The Image Bank/Eric Meola on page 126 (above); Simon Shepheard/Impact Photos on page 129 (below left); Barry Lewis/Network Photographers on page 114 (below); Pictor International on pages 121, 127; Spectrum Colour Library on page 120 (below); Tony Stone Images on page 129 (centre left); Wei Ming Tao on page 129 (centre right); Telegraph Colour Library/Stock Directory/VCL on page 120 (above); Nigel Webber on page 126 (below).

Picture research by Sandie Huskinson-Rolfe (PHOTOSEEKERS).

Book design by Peter Ducker MSTD.

To *the student*

This book is for candidates preparing for the University of Cambridge Certificate of Proficiency in English examination and provides practice in all the written and oral papers. It contains 5 complete tests, based on the Proficiency examinations set between 1992 and 1994. The examination consists of 5 papers, as follows:

Paper 1 Reading Comprehension (1 hour)
Section A consists of 25 multiple-choice items in the form of a sentence with a blank to be filled in by 1 of 4 words or phrases.
Section B consists of 15 multiple-choice items based on 3 or more reading passages of different types.
In the live examination, you will have to record your answers on a separate answer sheet. See page 133 for a sample answer sheet.

Paper 2 Composition (2 hours)
There are 5 topics from which you choose 2. The topics include discursive, descriptive and narrative essays, a directed writing exercise and an essay based on optional reading. (In these practice tests the questions based on optional reading are set on the kind of books that are prescribed each year. These are *not* the actual books prescribed for any particular year: they are just given as examples.)

Paper 3 Use of English (2 hours)
Section A contains exercises of various kinds which test your control of English usage and grammatical structure.
Section B consists of a passage followed by questions which test your comprehension and skill in summarising.

Paper 4 Listening Comprehension (about 35 minutes)
You answer a variety of questions on 3 or 4 recorded passages from English broadcasts, interviews, announcements, phone messages, conversations etc. Each passage is heard twice.
In the live examination, you will have to transfer your answers onto a separate answer sheet. See page 134 for a sample answer sheet.

Paper 5 Speaking Test (about 15 minutes)
You take part in a conversation based on a photograph, passage and other material from authentic sources linked by theme, either with a group of other candidates or with the examiner alone. The exercises in these tests include some of the type set in the examination on optional reading.

Practice Test 1

PAPER 1 READING COMPREHENSION   (1 hour)

There are **forty** questions on this paper. Attempt **all** questions. For each question there are four possible answers labelled **A, B, C** and **D**. Choose the **one** you consider correct and record your choice in **soft pencil** on the separate answer sheet.

Section A

In this section you must choose the word or phrase which best completes each sentence. **On your answer sheet**, indicate the letter **A, B, C** or **D** against the number of each item **1** to **25** for the word or phrase you choose. Give **one answer only** to each question.

1 This new glue is very useful for small repairs as it .... very rapidly.
   A thickens   **B** stiffens   **C** sets   **D** fixes

2 This rose was .... after the grower's grand-daughter.
   A distinguished   **B** renowned   **C** named   **D** identified

3 Advertisers often aim their campaigns at young people as they have considerable spending ....
   A power   **B** force   **C** energy   **D** ability

4 We've bought some .... chairs for the garden so that they are easy to store away.
   A adapting   **B** adjusting   **C** bending   **D** folding

5 Demand for the product is expected to peak five years from now and then to ....
   A taper off   **B** fall down   **C** set back   **D** drift away

6 We were working overtime to cope with a sudden .... in demand.
   A surge   **B** boost   **C** impetus   **D** thrust

7 Alan's photo was slightly too large for the frame so he decided to .... it.
   A hack   **B** chop   **C** slice   **D** trim

8 The area is famous for its .... gardens, where all kinds of different
   vegetables are grown.
   A market   **B** hothouse   **C** trade   **D** greenhouse

9 In court she was .... to have stolen company money.
   A claimed   **B** accused   **C** charged   **D** alleged

10 Although the patient received intensive treatment, there was no ....
   improvement in her condition.
   A decipherable   **B** legible   **C** discernible   **D** intelligible

11 The new speed restrictions were a .... debated issue.
   A heavily   **B** hotly   **C** deeply   **D** profoundly

12 Lack of sleep over the last few months is finally .... Jane.
   A catching up with   **B** getting on with   **C** coming over   **D** putting on

13 The train .... from side to side as it went round a series of bends.
   A turned   **B** curved   **C** lunged   **D** swayed

14 His change of job has .... him with a new challenge in life.
   A introduced   **B** initiated   **C** presented   **D** led

15 The prisoner made his escape under .... of darkness.
   A protection   **B** disguise   **C** cover   **D** cloak

16 That door is creaking again; it needs some oil on its ....
   A screws   **B** hinges   **C** nails   **D** joints

17 .... she's got a job that she likes, she's a lot happier.
   A Since when   **B** Just as   **C** Now that   **D** Just now

18 I don't want lots of excuses, I just want to hear the .... truth.
   A clear   **B** plain   **C** pure   **D** right

19 I didn't want to discuss the matter but he insisted on bringing it ....
   A up   **B** out   **C** about   **D** over

20 The suspect was deported to his own country to .... charges of fraud.
   A stand   **B** consider   **C** face   **D** defend

21 She .... to being a bit nervous about making her speech.
   A asserted   **B** confessed   **C** acknowledged   **D** granted

22 Before you sign the contract, ... in mind that you won't be able to change anything later.
  A bear   **B** hold   **C** retain   **D** reserve

23 No .... you're hungry if you haven't eaten since yesterday.
  A matter   **B** surprise   **C** wonder   **D** problem

24 She's more interested in job .... than in making a lot of money.
  A contentment   **B** satisfaction   **C** enjoyment   **D** pleasure

25 The local people are .... on the question of whether or not to support the plans for the airport.
  A disputed   **B** separated   **C** disagreed   **D** divided

Section B

In this section you will find after each of the passages a number of questions or unfinished statements about the passage, each with four suggested answers or ways of finishing. You must choose the one which you think fits best. **On your answer sheet**, indicate the letter **A**, **B**, **C** or **D** against the number of each item **26** to **40** for the answer you choose. Give **one answer only** to each question.

FIRST PASSAGE

By about ten thousand years ago, with virtually every part of the globe populated, however sparsely, humanity was in place for the advent of agriculture. At the time, hunting and gathering was the universal means of subsistence, each band of humans exploiting the seasonal offerings of the animal and plant kingdoms of its own locality. By now the bow and arrow had been invented, as had the spear and spearthrower; both of these were important technological advances for hunting. The technology of plant- and food-gathering, however, remained simple: merely a container in which to carry fruit, nuts and succulent roots back to the camp. Life was essentially nomadic, unhurried, leisurely.

In general, hunting and gathering bands were relatively small, consisting of perhaps five or six family units. They would be part of a large and widespread tribe, sharing the language and culture of their neighbours but subsisting as a small, mobile band. Some hunter-gatherers, however, did not have to move camp every few weeks in search of new food sources. Some even built small villages, containing a hundred or more people. The reason for this unusual stability would have been a particularly rich food source. One such village is in Lepenski Vir. There, on the eve of the agricultural revolution, a band of hunter-gatherers built a village perched above the rushing Danube. Although they gathered food from the surrounding countryside, their main subsistence was on fish from the river. In their village they carved faces on boulders, giving them distinctly fishy expressions.

An obvious first step from the straightforward gathering of abundant plant foods towards actually cultivating them is simply to help them grow a little better – by irrigation, for instance. Until not very long ago, the Paiute Indians of the Owens Valley in the south-western United States did just this. They dug irrigation canals which they fed from dammed streams to enhance the growth of their plant foods, none of which they planted themselves. Taking care of growing plants is certainly a step towards agriculture, but the distinctive element is the actual sowing of the seeds, and even more the sowing of specially selected seeds. The backbone of successful crop-growing has been genetic selection for high yield and for resistance to diseases.

Maize was one of the first crops to be cultivated, and the initial steps in the selective breeding towards today's super cob were probably fortuitous. The simple act of gathering the tiny cobs would tend to select those in which the kernels fall out least readily: if the cobs are taken back to the village to be dried, the kernels that survive the journey will be those which stick most tenaciously in the cob. Once people had taken the conscious step of sowing seeds it was then just a matter of experience and insight to improve the crops by using seeds from the healthiest plants of the previous season.

Whether, initially, deliberate sowing followed a conscious experiment, or was the result of keen observation of accidentally spilled seeds that had been meant for food, we shall never know. The event must have occurred independently in many places and in many different ways, sometimes perhaps accidentally and sometimes by design. And the circumstances for beginning regular root-cropping must also have differed. The previous focus of any hunting and gathering community must, of course, have influenced the style of agriculture it adopted.

26 At the time of the advent of agriculture, the global population
    A was restricted to particular types of land.
    B had begun to increase steadily.
    C was not evenly distributed.
    D had insufficient food supplies.

27 What characterised the finding of food at that time?
    A People's diet was varied throughout the year.
    B Hunters travelled long distances to stalk their prey.
    C Hunting was more significant than gathering.
    D What people ate depended on the time of year.

28 The writer mentions the people of Lepenski Vir because
    A they showed creative talent.
    B they caught fish.
    C they settled in one place.
    D they were among the first farmers.

29 What is the key element in the development of agriculture?
    A growing plants from specially chosen seed
    B taking care of growing plants
    C the channelling of water
    D finding plants that can resist disease

30 What first improved the quality of maize?
    A People chose which plants to collect.
    B It was a matter of chance.
    C Plants were carefully tended.
    D Farmers observed which plants did well.

SECOND PASSAGE

Brian Nichols, recently promoted Assistant Commissioner of Police, resented
Dalgliesh and found this dislike the more irritating because he wasn't sure that
it was justified. After twenty-five years of policing he regarded even his
antipathies with a judicial eye; he liked to be confident that the case against
the accused would stand up in court. With Dalgliesh he wasn't sure. Nichols
was the senior in rank but this gave him small satisfaction when he knew that
Dalgliesh could have outstripped him had he chosen. This lack of concern
about promotion, which Dalgliesh never condescended to justify, he saw as a
subtle criticism of his own more ambitious preoccupations. He deplored the
poetry, not on principle, but because it had conferred prestige and, therefore,
couldn't be regarded as a harmless hobby like fishing, gardening or
woodwork. A policeman, in his view, should be satisfied with policing. An
added grievance was that Dalgliesh chose most of his friends from outside
the force and those fellow officers he consorted with weren't always of an
appropriate rank. In a junior officer that would have been regarded as a
dangerous idiosyncrasy and in a senior it had a taint of disloyalty. And to
compound these delinquencies, he dressed too well. He was standing now
with easy assurance looking out of the window wearing a suit in a subtle
brown tweed which Nichols had seen him wearing for the last four years. It
bore the unmistakable stamp of an excellent tailor, probably, thought Nichols,
the firm his grandfather had patronised. Nichols, who enjoyed buying clothes,
sometimes with more enthusiasm than discrimination, felt that it was
becoming in a man to own rather more suits and those not so well tailored.
Finally, whenever he was with Dalgliesh, he felt inexplicably that he ought
perhaps to shave off his moustache and would find his hand moving
involuntarily to his upper lip as if to reassure himself that the moustache was
still a respectable appendage. This impulse, irrational, almost neurotic,
irritated him profoundly.
    Both men knew that Dalgliesh needn't be here in Nichols's tenth-floor
office, that the casual suggestion that the Assistant Commissioner should be
put in the picture was no more than an invitation, not a command. With the

5

Commissioner temporarily away at a conference, he could argue that he had a right at least to a brief progress report. But, irrationally, part of him wished that Dalgliesh had objected, had given him the excuse for one of those departmental wrangles which he provoked when the job offered less excitement than his restless spirit craved and which he was adept at winning.

31 How did Brian Nichols regard his own attitude to Dalgliesh?
  A He thought it was probably right.
  B He was ashamed of it.
  C He knew most people would agree with him.
  D He was annoyed by it.

32 Nichols believed Dalgliesh to be critical of him because
  A Dalgliesh was not as ambitious as he was.
  B Dalgliesh had a creative talent.
  C Dalgliesh wouldn't explain himself.
  D Dalgliesh was more famous than he was.

33 What bothered Nichols about Dalgliesh's circle of friends?
  A It included people from undesirable sectors of society.
  B It distracted him from his work.
  C It might compromise his professional position.
  D It raised questions about his commitment to the police.

34 How did Dalgliesh's appearance affect Nichols?
  A It caused him to question his own taste.
  B It made him feel jealous of Dalgliesh's family background.
  C It displeased him because Dalgliesh dressed inappropriately for a policeman.
  D It irritated him that Dalgliesh spent so little on clothes.

35 How had Dalgliesh reacted when asked to come to Nichols's office?
  A He had tried to find an excuse.
  B He had only come when ordered.
  C He had made no objection.
  D He had been involved in an argument about it.

THIRD PASSAGE

Gestures, by definition, transmit signals, and these signals must come across clearly if we are to understand their messages. They cannot afford to be vague and woolly; they must be crisp and sharp and difficult to confuse with other signals. To do this they have to develop a 'typical form' that shows comparatively little variation. And they must be performed with a 'typical intensity', showing much the same speed, strength and amplitude on each occasion that they are brought into action.

It is rather like the ringing of a telephone bell. The signal goes on sounding at fixed intervals, at a fixed volume, and with a fixed sound, no matter how urgent the call. No-one confuses a telephone bell with a front-door bell or an alarm clock. Its fixed form and its fixed intensity make it unmistakable.

The process is at work in human gestures. When an angry man shakes his fist, the chances are that the speed, force and amplitude of each shake, as the fist jerks back and forth in mid-air, are much the same on each occasion that he employs this gesture. And there is a reasonable likelihood that his speed, force and amplitude will be similar to those of any other fist-shaker. If, as an experiment, you were to perform a fist-shaking gesture in which you slowed down the movement, decreased the force, and increased the distance travelled by the clenched fist, it is doubtful if your signal would be understood. An onlooker might imagine you were exercising your arm, but it is doubtful if he would read the message as a threat display.

Most of our gestures have grown into typical presentations of this kind. We all wave in much the same way, clap our hands at roughly the same speed, beckon with much the same amplitude and shake our heads with much the same rhythm. This is not a conscious process. We simply tune in to the cultural norm. Unwittingly, we smooth the path of the hundreds of tiny messages that fly between us whenever we meet and interact. Somehow we manage to match up our gestures with those of our companions, and they do the same with ours. Together we all synchronise the intensities of our gesturing until we are all operating in concert, as if under the control of an invisible cultural conductor.

As always with human behaviour there are exceptions to this general rule. We are not automatons. We show personal idiosyncrasies – individual variations on the cultural themes. One man, with a particularly fine set of teeth, shows an exaggeratedly intense, open-lipped smile, and he does this even in mild situations. Another man, with bad teeth, gives a more closed smile, even when strongly stimulated. One man bellows with laughter, while another titters, in reaction to the same joke. These are Gesture Variants, and they provide each of us with a behavioural 'style', or body personality. They are small differences compared with our general gesture-conformity, but they can become important personal labels none the less.

36 What do successful gestures have in common?
  A speed
  B clarity
  C intensity
  D style

37 What characteristics do successful gestures share with telephone bells?
A They go on for a long time.
B It is not usual to mistake what they mean.
C They are repeated regularly.
D People know they must be responded to.

38 A fist-shaking gesture might cause confusion if
A the gesture didn't have the right rhythm.
B the person failed to synchronise his movement with those around him.
C the person also shook his head.
D the gesture was unusual for that particular person.

39 According to the passage, what makes people develop similar gestures?
A the need to be liked
B the desire to be part of a particular culture
C the need to facilitate communication
D the conscious desire to be like other people

40 What accounts for individual variation in gestures?
A people's desire to show off their good features
B the fact that people live in different cultures
C the fact that people are different shapes and sizes
D the need to develop one's own manner

PAPER 2 COMPOSITION   (2 hours)

Answer any **two** questions.
Your answers must follow exactly the instructions given.
Write your answers on the separate answer paper provided.
Write clearly in pen, not pencil. You may make alterations but make sure that your work is **easy to read.** Write both question numbers clearly in the left-hand margin at the beginning of your answers.

1   Describe a person whom you regard as successful and define the qualities needed to achieve success. (About 350 words)

2   Nowadays people live longer than they did in the past. Discuss the advantages of living longer and the problems created by this situation. (About 350 words)

3   Write a story entitled *The Lost Diary.* (About 350 words)

4   There has been considerable noise caused by low-flying aircraft over the area where you live. Write to the airport authorities to complain and to explain the effect of the noise on you and your neighbours. Suggest what actions the authorities could take and what compensation they should offer. (About 300 words)

5   Based on your reading of **one** of these books, write on **one** of the following. (About 350 words)

RUTH PRAWER JHABVALA: *Heat and Dust*
Discuss the reasons why Olivia left her husband and describe the effects this decision had on her family and friends.

TIMOTHY MO: *Sour Sweet*
Describe how Chen becomes involved with the Wo Society and comment on how this affects him.

WILLIAM GOLDING: *Lord of the Flies*
'Piggy is different from the other boys.' Use this statement to describe his character and the events which lead to his death.

PAPER 3 USE OF ENGLISH (2 hours)

Section A

1 Fill each of the numbered blanks in the passage with **one** suitable word.

Endangered species

The future of the African elephant depends on man. No **(1)** .... can human beings and wild animals live in harmony throughout vast areas of the continent **(2)** .... was possible in days gone **(3)** ...., for man's needs have increased as well as **(4)** .... numbers. There are regions, **(5)** .... as the Congo forests and the equatorial Sudan, **(6)** .... the old relationship may remain for a **(7)** .... more years or even generations, but in general it has gone. Conservation, **(8)** .... it is to be effective, **(9)** .... be a positive, constructive policy, and it is wishful thinking to imagine **(10)** ...., particularly in the case of the elephant. And if this is not yet true of the whole of Africa, **(11)** .... soon will be, for the increase **(12)** .... the human population is almost universal. Where human beings and wild animals find **(13)** .... in competition with **(14)** .... other, the animals will lose. Even if **(15)** .... appears to be enough room for both, man will not tolerate **(16)** .... long a situation in which elephants and other creatures make even occasional raids **(17)** .... his fields of food or economic crops. For many years **(18)** .... has been a major cause of conflicting interests and **(19)** .... of the reasons why so many elephants have been shot to control **(20)** .... numbers.

2 Finish each of the following sentences in such a way that it is **as similar as possible in meaning to the sentence printed before it**.

EXAMPLE: I expect that he will get there by lunchtime.

ANSWER: I expect him *to get there by lunchtime.*

a) I was amazed when Eva got into university, given the fact that she hadn't worked hard at school.

To my ....

....

b) Le Corbusier was very influential in developing architectural styles.

Le Corbusier had ....

....

c) She contributes with enthusiasm to class discussions.

Her ....

....

d) Tim insisted on being told the complete story.

Nothing but ....

....

e) The only thing that makes this job worthwhile is the money.

Were ....

....

f) Jane's husband will be returning from South America quite soon.

It won't ....

....

g) The council rarely allows appeals against its decisions.

Hardly ....

....

h) My brother-in-law is the most exasperating person I've ever met.

I've yet ....

....

3 Fill each of the blanks with a suitable word or phrase.

EXAMPLE: He doesn't mind one way or the other; it makes *no difference to* him.

a) The problem is that .... does always seems to land him in trouble.

b) Try .... sleep over it; everything will be all right in the end.

c) You .... sense than to buy Jack's old car without driving it first.

d) If you had been in my place, ... done?

e) A player was injured when the game .... progress for only a few minutes.

f) People on the poverty line find it hard to .... meet.

4 For each of the sentences below, write a new sentence **as similar as possible in meaning to the original sentence**, but using the word given. This word **must not be altered in any way**.

EXAMPLE: Not many people attended the meeting.
         turnout

ANSWER: *There was a poor turnout for the meeting.*

a) She has always had a good relationship with the children.
       got

....

....

b) Without skilful surgery he would not have survived the operation.
       thanks

....

....

c) You'd feel better if you had a quiet holiday.
do

....

....

d) With six children to look after, she's extremely busy.
hands

....

....

e) There's no point in your phoning Caroline – she's away.
time

....

....

f) What Rachel does in her spare time doesn't concern me.
business

....

....

g) Only final-year students are allowed to use the main college car park.
restricted

....

....

h) The final version of the plan was quite different from the initial draft.
resemblance

....

....

Section B

5   Read this passage, then answer the questions which follow it.

Computers on the phone

The phone rings as you are rushing to get ready for work. When you snatch up the receiver, the disembodied voice at the other end tells you slowly that double-glazing in your area has been reduced to half price for a limited period. It continues this litany unruffled through angry curses that would have dispatched the most thick-skinned tele-sales person. 5 That's because it's a computer.

This nightmarish prospect has already been partly realised in the United States, where those who have found it unendurable have been installing telephone answering machines – even though that might filter out the wanted as well as the unwanted calls.   10

Scientists, who see advances in computer technology as synonymous with progress, argue that they have given us rapid access to information such as bank account details. Booking holidays, airline seats and theatre tickets is much quicker and simpler than in pre-computer days. But talking computers open up a less agreeable dimension. A 15 computerised sales representative is impervious to the most intemperate language. Nor does it have a sense of embarrassment because it has called at a moment of maximum inconvenience. In fact, it may call back at a similarly inconvenient time again … and again.

Some victims of the US tele-sales computer are left wondering what 20 technological misery comes next. Now the answer seems clear: the computerised conversationalist. Developments in speech-processing mean that computers may soon be able to hold a simple conversation. Instead of simply dialling up subscribers and repeating computerised messages, they will perhaps be able to receive, understand and answer 25 basic enquiries.

The commercial advantages of replacing humans with computers are obvious, even if the benefits for people are questionable. From the employer's point of view, the computer does not make excessive claims for its abilities at a job interview, pinch pens or office stationery, or 30 take breaks for coffee, lunch or tea. It is never unpleasant to customers, even when provoked, nor ineffectual because of tiredness or a heavy hangover.

A single machine can take the place of dozens of sales people, and yet uses little more than the equivalent of two desk spaces. It has enough 35 intelligence to do the job, but not so much that it becomes troublesome when another machine is assigned more important work: much managerial time is saved in not having to appease dissatisfied workers. It costs nothing in health insurance, cannot be sexually harassed and can

be replaced, without redundancy payments, as soon as a more efficient 40
model comes on the market.

The chief problem is that commercial pressures may force computers
onto the market long before the technology is available to give them the
ability to converse intelligently with the public. If, for example, a traveller
rings the railway station and asks in a clear voice when the next train is, 45
the computer should be able to answer. If customers want to know if the
trains are running on time or whether it is possible to get a refund on an
unused ticket, they may encounter difficulty.

a) Explain what 'disembodied voice' means in this context. (line 2)

....

....

b) What is 'this litany' and why is it 'unruffled'? (line 4)

....

....

c) Explain in your own words what effect 'angry curses' would have had on a
'thick-skinned tele-sales person'. (lines 4–5)

....

....

d) How have some people reacted to computerised tele-sales in the USA?

....

....

e) What does the writer mean by 'impervious to the most intemperate
language'? (lines 16–17)

....

....

f) How might a computer show its insensitivity when it had inconvenienced a
customer?

....

....

g) Who are the 'victims', referred to in line 20?

....

....

h) What development in tele-sales computers does the writer anticipate?

....

....

i) Mention two human weaknesses that would be avoided if people were replaced by computers.

....

....

j) Name one immediate financial saving for the employer on installing a computer.

....

....

k) Explain what is meant by 'not having to appease dissatisfied workers'. (line 38)

....

....

l) Why might these computers come onto the market before they are capable of intelligent conversation?

....

....

m) What type of enquiry would such a computer be able to handle initially?

....

....

n) In a paragraph of 70-90 words, describe the advantages of computer tele-sales to the employer, and their disadvantages to the customer.

....

....

....

....

....

....

....

....

....

....

....

....

....

....

PAPER 4 LISTENING COMPREHENSION (about 35 minutes)

In the live examination, you will have to transfer your answers to the separate answer sheet. See page 134 for a sample answer sheet.

PART ONE

You will hear a radio interview with James Evans about so-called environmentally friendly products. James Evans is a member of Friends of the Earth, an organisation that takes an interest in the environment and conservation. For questions **1-4**, indicate which of the alternatives **A**, **B**, **C** or **D** is the most appropriate response.

(When transferring your answers, write A, B, C or D on the answer sheet.)

1 The attitude of Friends of the Earth to the new 'green' products is

    A shocked.

    B pleased.

    C concerned.

    D angry.

A	
B	
C	
D	

2 Friends of the Earth give an annual award called

    A the Friends of the Earth award.

    B the Green Con of the year.

    C the great green logo.

    D the BNF elimination prize.

A	
B	
C	
D	

3 Why do Friends of the Earth want a government labelling scheme?

    A to make Great Britain the same as Canada and Japan

    B to give consumers confidence in what they buy

    C to penalise companies who make false claims

    D to increase public awareness

A	
B	
C	
D	

4 A green logo shows that a product

    A has passed an independent test.

    B has been approved by the Consumers Association.

    C is promoted by Friends of the Earth.

    D claims to be environmentally friendly.

A	
B	
C	
D	

PART TWO

You will hear an interview between a researcher doing a public opinion survey and a passer-by. The researcher is interested in information and opinions about the shops in Farley Road. Look at the form which the interviewer uses. For questions **5-15**, complete the form by circling the appropriate response, and for questions **16** and **17**, by writing down what the passer-by mentions.

(When transferring your answers, write A, B, C or D; or Y or N; or a word or short phrase, as appropriate, on the answer sheet.)

TOWN PLANNING DEPARTMENT
PUBLIC OPINION SURVEY

Farley Road Shops Redevelopment Scheme – Phase One

5   Do you use the shops in Farley Road?   YES/NO

6   If yes, what do you use them for?   (CIRCLE)

    A   All your groceries   **C**   Only fruit
    B   Occasional items   **D**   Only vegetables

7   If yes to question 5, how would you rate their goods for range and quality?

    A Excellent   **B** Good   **C** Fair   **D** Poor

ALL INTERVIEWEES: If a supermarket were to be built, which of the following would improve?

(CIRCLE)

8 Service	YES/NO	**12** Quality of merchandise	YES/NO
9 Range	YES/NO	**13** Opening hours	YES/NO
10 Prices	YES/NO	**14** Hygiene	YES/NO
11 Time-saving	YES/NO	**15** Personal contact	YES/NO

ALL INTERVIEWEES: List briefly what <u>problems</u> you think might be caused by a supermarket:

16

17

PART THREE

You will hear an extract from a radio programme, in which a woman explains how a miners' strike is affecting life for miners and their families. For questions **18-21**, indicate which of the alternatives **A**, **B**, **C** or **D** is the most appropriate response.

(When transferring your answers, write A, B, C or D on the answer sheet.)

18 Which <u>items</u> are considered basic necessities in the weekly food parcels?

A	
B	
C	
D	

   A fruit and meat

   B vegetables and sugar

   C sugar and tea

   D vegetables and meat

19 The woman describes the incident involving the <u>shoes</u> to illustrate

   A how generous people are.

   B how desperate things are.

   C how fast boys grow.

   D how close the community is.

A	
B	
C	
D	

20 The prospect of permanent unemployment alarms the woman because it will mean

   A being short of money.

   B constant family quarrels.

   C the possibility of violence.

   D a loss of morale.

A	
B	
C	
D	

21 The woman's tone is

   A determined.

   B resigned.

   C bitter.

   D aggressive.

A	
B	
C	
D	

PART FOUR

You will hear the Principal of Sturton College of Art taking some prospective students on a tour of the college. For questions **22-30**, indicate the correct response by ⟨circling⟩ TRUE or FALSE.

(When transferring your answers, write T or F on the answer sheet.)

22 The guide blames other members of staff for the late start.   TRUE/FALSE

23 The guide feels that the tour may not interest all the students.   TRUE/FALSE

24 Jenny thinks her students have excellent facilities.   TRUE/FALSE

25 Jenny hopes students will bring one of their sculptures to
the interview.   TRUE/FALSE

26 The students themselves have painted the walls of the
painting room.   TRUE/FALSE

27 Denis thought that the computer room was open.   TRUE/FALSE

28 Michael was expecting to help with the tour.   TRUE/FALSE

29 Each student has exclusive use of a computer.   TRUE/FALSE

30 Graphic Design students need previous commercial
experience.   TRUE/FALSE

PAPER 5 SPEAKING TEST   (about 15 minutes)

You will be asked to take part in a conversation with a group of other students or with your teacher. The conversation will be based on one particular topic area or theme, for example education, problems in society, the arts.

Of course each Speaking Test will be different for each student or group of students, but a *typical* test is described below.

★ At the start of the Speaking Test you will be asked to talk about one of the photographs among the Exercises on pages 114–116 at the back of the book; more than simple descriptions will be required.

★ You will then be asked to discuss one of the passages at the back of the book. Your teacher may ask you to talk about its content, where you think it comes from, who the author or speaker is, whether you agree or disagree with it, and so on. You will *not* be asked to read the passage aloud, but you may quote parts of it to make your point.

★ You may then be asked to discuss, for example, an advertisement, a leaflet, an extract from a newspaper, a quotation, etc. Your teacher will tell you which of the Speaking Test Exercises to look at.

★ You may also be asked to take part in an activity with a group of other students or your teacher which is intended to test your ability to interact successfully with other speakers during conversation and discussion in English. Your teacher will tell you which section among the Speaking Test Exercises you should look at.

Practice Test 2

PAPER 1 READING COMPREHENSION (1 hour)

There are **forty** questions on this paper. Attempt **all** questions. For each question there are four possible answers labelled **A**, **B**, **C** and **D**. Choose the **one** you consider correct and record your choice in **soft pencil** on the separate answer sheet.

Section A

In this section you must choose the word or phrase which best completes each sentence. **On your answer sheet**, indicate the letter **A**, **B**, **C** or **D** against the number of each item **1** to **25** for the word or phrase you choose. Give **one answer only** to each question.

1 Several passengers received minor injuries when the train unexpectedly came
   to a ....
   A delay   **B** stand   **C** brake   **D** halt

2 John refused to put his career in .... by opposing his boss.
   A jeopardy   **B** hazard   **C** risk   **D** stake

3 Angela's work was praised for its .... attention to detail.
   A meticulous   **B** significant   **C** subtle   **D** concentrated

4 Motorists should .... well in advance of changing lanes.
   A sign   **B** signal   **C** flare   **D** flicker

5 The student had no money left and took out a loan to .... him over until
   the end of term.
   A last   **B** tend   **C** keep   **D** tide

6 The climbers sought .... from the storm.
   A escape   **B** refuge   **C** solace   **D** defence

7 The tour guide had a brightly-coloured company badge pinned to the
   .... of her jacket.
   A lapel   **B** border   **C** edge   **D** hem

8 It was her first conference as party leader, and she was determined to .... her authority on the proceedings.
A press   **B** thrust   **C** stamp   **D** mark

9 It was .... of a surprise to Andrew that he got the job.
A rather   **B** something   **C** quite   **D** much

10 The last bus had gone so we were .... with the problem of how to get home that night.
A affronted   **B** caught   **C** trapped   **D** faced

11 I don't want to go into all the details about why I left: .... it to say that I had a better offer from another company.
A take   **B** grant   **C** give   **D** suffice

12 Finish your meal with a cup of our delicious freshly .... coffee.
A grated   **B** ground   **C** shredded   **D** minced

13 At the most important stage of the season, the footballer was troubled by the .... of an old injury.
A recurrence   **B** renewal   **C** restart   **D** resumption

14 The pianist played beautifully, showing a real .... for the music.
A sense   **B** understanding   **C** sentiment   **D** feeling

15 Rachel painted a gloomy .... of life as a student.
A image   **B** picture   **C** drawing   **D** illustration

16 With its engine disabled, the fishing vessel was at the .... of the storm.
A whim   **B** mercy   **C** control   **D** grip

17 The more expensive carpet is a good choice .... it will last longer.
A by means of   **B** due to   **C** in that   **D** in view of

18 Money was short and people survived by .... and saving.
A scrimping   **B** scavenging   **C** scouring   **D** scrounging

19 The company had severe problems and the board decided to .... it up.
A fold   **B** close   **C** wind   **D** put

20 It is with .... regret that we have to inform you that your scholarship has been withdrawn.
A heavy   **B** sombre   **C** deep   **D** high

21 Nobody .... him winning the award, so it came as a big surprise.
A foresaw   **B** dreamt   **C** predicted   **D** forecast

22 Marianne seemed to take .... at my comments on her work.
    A annoyance   **B** insult   **C** offence   **D** indignation

23 The candidate still expects to be re-elected .... the results of the latest opinion poll.
    A without   **B** apart   **C** nevertheless   **D** notwithstanding

24 The actor never .... the potential he showed in his early career.
    A fulfilled   **B** assumed   **C** gained   **D** accomplished

25 I didn't set .... to start an argument, it just happened.
    A off   **B** out   **C** about   **D** up

Section B

In this section you will find after each of the passages a number of questions or unfinished statements about the passage, each with four suggested answers or ways of finishing. You must choose the one which you think fits best. **On your answer sheet**, indicate the letter **A**, **B**, **C** or **D** against the number of each item **26** to **40** for the answer you choose. Give **one answer only** to each question.

FIRST PASSAGE

From its foundation in 1984 English Heritage has been an organisation which has recognised the need to provide guidance for others on good conservation practice. Now, the organisation has published *The Repair of Historic Buildings: advice on principles and methods,* a book that sets out the principles and methods that the group believes should be applied in the repair of historic buildings and monuments.

The primary purpose of repair, it says, is to restrain the process of decay without damaging the character of buildings or monuments, altering the features that give them their historic or architectural importance, or unnecessarily disturbing or destroying historic fabric. In short, the goal is to conserve as found.

The importance of understanding the historical development of a building and of making records of this before and during repairs is stressed. So too is the need to analyse carefully and monitor existing defects before deciding on solutions. Existing materials and methods of construction should normally be matched in repairs, except where defects have clearly been caused by faulty specifications or design. In such cases, traditional alternatives are preferred to more recently developed and insufficiently proven techniques. Additions or alterations to a building are often important for the way they illustrate historical development. So they should be retained. There are cases where later changes detract from, rather than add to, the interest of the original, but it is now recognised by most that the restorations are important phases in the history of a building. Today, restoration back to the original structure is rare, usually only attempted when sufficient evidence exists, and where the later work is undisputedly of poor quality.

For practical measures, the book advises, the first line of defence is day-to-day maintenance that can be done by the owner of the building. This will include keeping gutters and rainwater pipes clear, removing vegetation and ensuring there is adequate ventilation. Then there is maintenance in the form of minor repairs – which usually requires the services of a builder. The longest section of the book discusses techniques of repair for each of the main elements and associated materials ranging from structural stabilisation to applying internal finishes such as plain and decorative plasterwork.

Inevitably there are techniques that are currently the subject of research, and alternatives to traditional methods which may be promising, but which have not yet been well proven. There are matters of approach about which there have long been differences of opinion among conservationists. But English Heritage intends to revise the book to take account of such developments.

Opinions differ more about the approach to repairing stonework than about almost any other element of a historic building. In the case of valuable medieval fabric, especially where there is carved work, the object should be to conserve and consolidate what is there, and replace the bare minimum. For general stonework repairs, decisions on the extent of replacement can be the subject of strong debate. Generally, English Heritage advises, stones of medieval buildings should only be replaced where they have lost their structural integrity because of deep erosion, or because of serious fracturing. A different approach may be appropriate for classical or Gothic revival buildings, particularly if they are the work of important architects and if there is a need to retain the integrity and clarity of design.

Debate of this kind will always continue to exercise the minds of conservationists. For this reason there can never be a standard specification for the repair and conservation of historic buildings.

26 The new book suggests that, when restoring a building, it is important to
   A employ experts throughout the work.
   B emphasise the character of the building.
   C keep accurate records of the work.
   D conceal damaged sections from view.

27 Alternative building materials are only recommended if
   A the original choice was unsuitable.
   B the building has developed defects.
   C traditional materials are unavailable.
   D the appearance of the building will not be affected.

28 Later additions to buildings should be removed if they are
   A intended to hide original features.
   B badly constructed.
   C in an inferior style.
   D in different materials from the original construction.

29 What is English Heritage's attitude to new repair techniques?
   A They are an improvement on traditional methods.
   B They should only be used as a last resort.
   C They should be treated with caution.
   D They stimulate useful discussion.

30 Medieval stonework should be replaced only if
   A it has no carving on it.
   B it has suffered severe cracking.
   C its condition is affecting the foundations.
   D it was not part of the architect's design.

SECOND PASSAGE

Alone in the apartment, Polly continued typing for ten minutes, then stopped to reheat her coffee. For the first time she felt the disadvantages of having become Jeanne's room mate. She didn't like being blamed for not wanting to visit Ida and Cathy, who weren't really her friends, and would probably be happier if she didn't come so they could analyse her character the way they always did with people who weren't there. They talked in a kind of catty way, even in a bitchy way. Polly scowled, catching herself in a lapse of language. Jeanne, among others, had often pointed out how unfair it was that when women were compared to animals it was always unfavourably: *catty, cow, henpecked*. While for men the comparison was usually positive: *strong as a bull, cock of the walk*.

She turned on the tape recorder again and typed another page, then stopped, thinking of Jeanne again. She didn't like being called a workaholic, even affectionately. She didn't like being given permission not to see people she didn't want to see. It was, yes, as if she were a child, with a managing, overprotective mother.

Of course, when she really was a child, Polly never had an overprotective mother. Bea was only twenty when her daughter was born and she'd had trouble enough protecting herself. She looked out for Polly the way an older sister or a baby-sitter might have done, without anxiety, encouraging her to become independent as fast as possible. Later, when Polly's half-brothers came along, Bea had shown impulses towards overprotection, but her husband frustrated them; he didn't want his sons 'made into sissies'.

According to Elsa, Polly's former shrink, any close relationship between women could revive one's first and profoundest attachment, to one's mother.

Physically, of course, Jeanne was nothing like Polly's mother. Bea Milner was much smaller, for one thing. But to a child, all grown women are large. And psychologically there were similarities: Jeanne, like Bea, was soft and feminine in manner and given to gently chiding Polly for her impulsiveness, hot temper and lack of tact. Elsa's view had been that Polly needed Jeanne to play this role because she hadn't had enough 'good mothering' as a child and that Jeanne needed to play it because she was a highly maternal woman without children.

But I'm not a child any more, Polly thought. I don't want mothering. Anyhow, I'm four years older than Jeanne; the whole idea is stupid. She poured her coffee and added less sugar than usual.

31 What did Polly resent?
  A Jeanne's attitude to her
  B Ida and Cathy's gossip
  C having to share a room
  D being talked about

32 Why did Polly scowl?
  A because she disliked Ida and Cathy
  B because she wouldn't be missed
  C because Jeanne had criticised the language she used
  D because she was irritated by the words she was using

33 What do we learn about Polly's childhood?
  A She had felt a lack of affection.
  B She had learned to look after herself.
  C She was often separated from her mother.
  D She resented the attention her half-brothers received.

34 Which of her step-father's opinions does Polly recall?
  A Boys need to be self-reliant.
  B Mothers should treat all their children in the same way.
  C Girls are more emotional than boys.
  D Children should not be treated with affection.

35 In what respect did Jeanne resemble Polly's mother?
  A her impatience
  B her appearance
  C her manner of speaking
  D her level of intelligence

THIRD PASSAGE

There is no doubt that aggression and territoriality are part of modern life: vandalism is a distressingly familiar mark of the urban scene; we lock the doors of our houses and apartments against strangers who might wander in; and there is war, an apparent display of territoriality and aggression on a grand scale. Are these unsavoury aspects of modern living simply part of an inescapable legacy of our animal origins? Or are they phenomena with entirely different causes? These are questions that must be answered since they are so clearly relevant to the future of our species.

To begin with, it is worth taking a broad view of territoriality and aggression in the animal world. Why are some animals territorial? Simply to protect resources, such as food, a nest, or a similar reproductive area. Many birds defend one piece of real estate in which a male may attract and court a female, and then move off to another one, also to be defended, in which they build a nest and rear young. The 'choking' by male kittiwakes, the lunging by sticklebacks, and the early morning chorus by gibbons are all displays announcing ownership of territory. Intruders who persist in violating another's territory are soon met with such displays, the intention of which is quite clear. The clarity of the defender's response, and also of the intruder's prowess, is the secret of nature's success with these so-called aggressive encounters.

Such confrontations are strictly ritualised, so that on all but the rarest occasions the biologically fitter of the two wins without the infliction of physical damage on either one. This 'aggression' is in fact an exercise in competitive display rather than physical violence. The individuals engage in stereotyped lunges, thrusts, and postures which may or may not be similar to their responses when a real threat to their lives arises, as from a predator, for instance. In either event, the outcome is a resolution of a territorial dispute with minimal injury to either party. The biological advantage of these mock battles is clear: a species that insists on settling disputes violently reduces its overall fitness to thrive in a world that offers enough environmental challenges anyway.

The biological common sense implicit in this simple behavioural device is reiterated again and again throughout the animal kingdom, and even as far down as some ants. This law is so deeply embedded in the nature of survival and success in the game of evolution that for a species to transgress, there must be extremely unusual circumstances. We cannot deny that with the invention of tools, first made of wood and later of stone, an impulse to employ them occasionally as weapons might have caused serious injury, there being no stereotyped behaviour patterns to deflect their risk. And it is possible that our increasingly intelligent ancestors may have understood the implications of power over others through the delivery of one swift blow with a sharpened pebble tool. But is it likely?

The answer must be no. An animal that develops a proclivity for killing its fellows thrusts itself into a disadvantageous evolutionary position. Because our ancestors probably lived in small bands, in which individuals were closely related to one another, and had as neighbours similar bands which also contained blood relatives, in most acts of murder the victim would more than likely have been kin to the murderer. As evolutionary success is the production of as many descendants as possible, an innate drive for killing individuals of one's own species would soon have wiped that species out. Humans, as we know, did not blunder up an evolutionary blind alley, a fate that innate, unrestrained aggressiveness would undoubtedly have produced.

36 The writer considers it important to determine the reasons for aggression in modern life because
   A he wants to stress our links with animals.
   B vandalism is unpleasant.
   C future generations may be affected.
   D personal safety has become an issue.

37 Animals are territorial because
   A they have to protect their offspring.
   B nests are needed for different purposes.
   C they are naturally aggressive.
   D there is a limited supply of things they need.

38 In territorial confrontations, physical damage is
   A usually what happens in the end.
   B a consequence of competitive display.
   C inflicted to indicate superior status.
   D unlikely to happen in mock battles.

39 Physical damage is likely to occur during
   A courtship rituals.
   B conflict with a predator.
   C encounters between aggressive males.
   D the search for food.

40 What is the mark of evolutionary success for a species?
   A gaining control over a larger area
   B developing superior methods of attack
   C destroying all potential enemies
   D increasing the size of the population

PAPER 2 COMPOSITION   (2 hours)

Answer any **two** questions.
Your answers must follow exactly the instructions given.
Write your answers on the separate answer paper provided.
Write clearly in pen, not pencil. You may make alterations but make sure that your
work is **easy to read.** Write both question numbers clearly in the left-hand margin at
the beginning of your answers.

1   Describe a visit to a restaurant in your country and give your impressions of the
    atmosphere, decor and food. (About 350 words)

2   'National character and life-style are largely determined by climate.' Do you
    agree? (About 350 words)

3   Write a story ending with the words: *I heard the clock strike and I knew it was
    too late.* (About 350 words)

4   The school or college you have been attending has asked you, as a successful
    language learner, to write a piece for the student information booklet entitled
    'Helping Yourself to Learn'. Include any advice which you think would be of
    benefit to future students in helping them to improve their English language
    skills. (About 300 words)

5   Based on your reading of **one** of these books, write on **one** of the following.
    (About 350 words)

    HARPER LEE: *To Kill a Mocking Bird*
    '... *your pa's not a run-of-the-mill man ...*' How does Atticus differ from the
    residents of Maycomb county in his attitude and actions?

    TIMOTHY MO: *Sour Sweet*
    '*So, again, the household, presented with change and challenge, poured itself
    around the problem, dissolved what it was able to and absorbed what it could
    not.*' Show how the Chen family cope with a number of problems.

    WILLIAM GOLDING: *Lord of the Flies*
    What attempts do the boys make to establish order on the island and why do
    these attempts fail?

PAPER 3 USE OF ENGLISH (2 hours)

Section A

1   Fill each of the numbered blanks in the passage with **one** suitable word.

Illiteracy

Illiteracy may be considered more as an abstract concept than a condition. When a famous English writer used **(1)** .... word over two hundred years ago, he was actually **(2)** .... to people who could **(3)** .... read Greek or Latin. **(4)** ...., it seems unlikely that university examiners had **(5)** .... sort of disability in **(6)** .... when they reported on 'creeping illiteracy' in a report on their students' final examination in 1988.

Over the years, university lecturers have **(7)** .... aware of an increasing tendency **(8)** .... grammatical sloppiness, poor spelling and general imprecision in their students' ways **(9)** .... writing; and sloppy writing is all **(10)** .... often a reflection of sloppy thinking. Their complaint was that they had **(11)** .... to do teaching their own subject **(12)** .... teaching their undergraduates to write.

Some lecturers believe that they have **(13)** .... duty to stress the importance of maintaining standards of clear thinking **(14)** .... the written word in a world dominated **(15)** .... visual communications and images. They **(16)** .... on the connection between clear thinking and a form of writing that is not **(17)** .... clear, but also sensitive to subtleties of meaning. The same lecturers argue that undergraduates appear to **(18)** .... the victims of a 'softening process' that begins with the teaching of English in schools, but this point of **(19)** .... has, not surprisingly, caused a great **(20)** .... of controversy.

2 Finish each of the following sentences in such a way that it is **as similar as possible in meaning to the sentence printed before it**.

EXAMPLE: Immediately after his arrival things went wrong.

ANSWER: No sooner *had he arrived than things went wrong.*

a) I have called this meeting in order to present the latest sales figures.

My purpose ....

b) Skyscrapers in the USA are on average taller than anywhere else in the world.

The average ....

c) I was surprised at how easy he was to talk to.

I hadn't expected ....

d) Experts think that all dogs evolved from wolves.

All dogs are ....

e) The two sides never looked likely to reach an agreement.

At no time ....

f) The permit expires at the end of this month.

The permit is not ....

g) I fully intend to find out who is responsible for the graffiti.

I have every ....

h) Absolute secrecy was crucial to the success of the mission.

Without ....

3 Fill each of the blanks with a suitable word or phrase.

> EXAMPLE: He doesn't mind one way or the other; it makes *no difference to* him.

a) If .... the road-works, we'd have got there on time.

b) Your neighbour's quarrels have .... with you, so don't get involved.

c) Whether or not Jim gets the job will .... he makes at the interview.

d) The fact that he had been ill at the time of the crime

.... account by the judge.

e) Over the years the theatre foyer has come .... as a meeting-place.

f) It's high time .... police what really happened.

4 For each of the sentences below, write a new sentence **as similar as possible in meaning to the original sentence**, but using the word given. This word **must not be altered in any way**.

> EXAMPLE: Not many people attended the meeting.
> **turnout**
>
> ANSWER: *There was a poor turnout for the meeting.*

a) His irresponsible attitude is endangering his career as a doctor.
jeopardy

....

....

b) He got married without his parents' knowledge.
unaware

....

....

c) The incident ruined my chances of promotion.
paid

....

....

d) They wouldn't let the former chairman attend the conference.
barred

....

....

e) They feel the same way about each other.
mutual

....

....

f) I find Harold's behaviour quite incomprehensible.
loss

....

....

g) The orchestra is looking for alternative accommodation.
else

....

....

h) On my birthday I had only my cat for company.
own

....

....

Section B

5 Read this passage, then answer the questions which follow it.

'Keep Everest tidy!'

Last summer, the British climber Chris Bonington and a small film crew went to the base camp of Nanga Parbat – one of the most spectacular and challenging peaks in the Himalayas – to make a film about the history of mountaineering. What they found was an outrage of modern times.

The camp, at the side of the Diamir face, had been transformed from 5 a grassy alpine oasis into a rubbish dump. In a letter to the world's climbing press, Bonington wrote: 'It was a huge rubbish tip with discarded tins and packaging scattered across the grass, piled into gullies, and stuffed under boulders, in a fearful mess. A few charred piles showed where someone had lit a fire, but had left the debris. Most refuse 10 had just been dumped. We cleared, crushed, burnt and buried ten barrels full – but there was much more to do.'

In the last few years, several expeditions have been mounted to clean up the debris of their predecessors. Last summer, a team of climbers organised by the Italian-based pressure group *Mountain Wilderness* 15 cleaned up Pakistan's K2 – the world's second highest peak. Tonnes of rubbish were collected and taken to a specially installed recycling machine at the town of Skardu.

Mountain Wilderness wanted to take tough action before it was too late. It urged Pakistan's government to set up baggage control checks, 20 and to require a refundable fee for every kilo of non-consumable baggage – which would be returned when that baggage was safely taken out of the country. It also suggested that subsequent expeditions be responsible for collecting equipment discarded in emergency situations. Failure to enforce these rules, said *Mountain Wilderness*, should be met with an 25 expedition boycott.

Others contest such a tough line. Lord Hunt – leader of the first successful expedition to the summit of Everest – made his views clear in a speech to the British Mountaineering Council (BMC) conference in March. 'The real safeguard for mountains and other areas of wild and 30 beautiful landscape lies not so much in rules and regulations as in education,' he said.

Rubbish is unsightly, but it is not the only evidence that mountaineering expeditions can have an impact on the environment. Nor is it the most serious. Erosion is a growing problem as more and more 35 trekking expeditions visit countries like Nepal. The erosion is caused by a combination of trampling boots and cutting down trees for fuel. The country's rapidly growing population has by far the greatest impact, but trekkers and expeditions exacerbate the problem in more remote areas.

Chris Bonington believes that change must be effected through elected national bodies, which would work closely with the governments of countries hosting expeditions. 'Climbers do need to come up with a code of conduct,' he says. 'This is being discussed and a lot of immensely well-intentioned groups are involved. But what we need is a co-ordinated international effort. The Union of International Alpine Associations (UIAA) is best qualified to come up with a solution because it is a democratically representative body.' Meanwhile, the BMC is drawing up its own guidelines, adherence to which will be a condition for grant aid for British expeditions in the future. Expeditions to any environment can leave trails of damage, wittingly or unwittingly, but it seems that climbers may, at last, be coming to grips with the impact of expeditions.

a) What is meant in the text by the phrase 'an outrage of modern times'? (line 4)

....

....

b) What had Chris Bonington been expecting to find at the base camp?

....

....

c) Mention two ways in which refuse had been concealed near the Diamir face.

....

....

d) Who does the word 'predecessors' refer to in line 14?

....

....

e) What technique did the *Mountain Wilderness* expedition use in their work on K2?

....

....

f) What would be the purpose of the 'refundable fee' proposed by *Mountain Wilderness*?

....

....

g) When might expeditions justifiably leave material behind?

....

....

h) In your own words, explain what action *Mountain Wilderness* proposed if new rules were not introduced.

....

....

i) How does Lord Hunt's position compare with that of *Mountain Wilderness*?

....

....

j) In your own words, explain how Lord Hunt compares 'education' with 'regulations'.

....

....

k) What is meant by a 'code of conduct' in line 43 and who would it affect?

....

....

l) What action will the BMC take against British expeditions which do not follow its new guidelines?

....

....

m) Explain in your own words how mountaineers' attitudes are currently changing.

....

....

n) In a paragraph of 70-90 words, state what problems have been caused by expeditions to remote areas and how they might be dealt with.

....

....

....

....

....

....

....

....

....

....

....

....

....

....

PAPER 4 · LISTENING COMPREHENSION (about 35 minutes)

In the live examination, you will have to transfer your answers to the separate answer sheet. See page 134 for a sample answer sheet.

PART ONE

You will hear an interview with Bernice, who is in her thirties. She is talking about her return to full-time studying after a number of years at home. For questions **1-5**, indicate which of the alternatives **A**, **B**, **C** or **D** is the most appropriate response.

(When transferring your answers, write A, B, C or D on the answer sheet.)

1   Why did Bernice decide to return to full-time study?

    A   She needed to help her children with their work.

    B   She wanted to understand the work her children were doing.

    C   She recognised an inner drive to learn more herself.

    D   She knew she was wasting her time at home.

A	
B	
C	
D	

2   'New Directions for Women' is a course which

    A   trains women for new careers in industry.

    B   supports women seeking a fresh start.

    C   prepares women to take new examinations.

    D   offers women a different work programme.

A	
B	
C	
D	

3   Bernice is currently on a course which

    A   is designed to train her in study skills.

    B   helps students cope with academic studies.

    C   caters for full-time students.

    D   occupies her for four days a week.

A	
B	
C	
D	

4 In the long term, Bernice hopes to

A work as a career adviser with mature students.

B become a career adviser for people made redundant.

C go into teaching at secondary level.

D train as a career adviser with adolescents.

A	
B	
C	
D	

5 Now that she is studying, Bernice finds it difficult to

A get down to a domestic routine.

B find time to look after the family.

C be relaxed over mundane domestic jobs.

D impose an academic routine on herself.

A	
B	
C	
D	

PART TWO

You will hear a talk about a person who was important in the history of navigation. For questions **6-15**, complete the notes.

(When transferring your answers, write the number, word or short phrase, as appropriate, on the answer sheet.)

6 John Harrison was born in [   ] **6**

7 How did he learn about clock-making?

	7

8 What were his clocks used to develop?

	8

9 What affected the accuracy of clocks at sea?

	9

10 What did the government committee propose for clock-makers?

	10

11 What was another name for marine chronometer?

	11

12 What did Harrison decide against using in his clocks?

	12

13 What did Harrison present to the committee?

	13

14 How many times was Harrison's invention officially tested?

	14

15 What did Harrison receive when he was over 80?

	15

PART THREE

Look at the plan of Compton Park Zoo. You will hear an announcement describing what's on at the zoo. For questions **16-25**, mark the mentioned attractions in their correct places on the plan, together with any times mentioned. Some have already been filled in for you.

(When transferring your answers, write the word or phrase, or leave blank, as appropriate, on the answer sheet.)

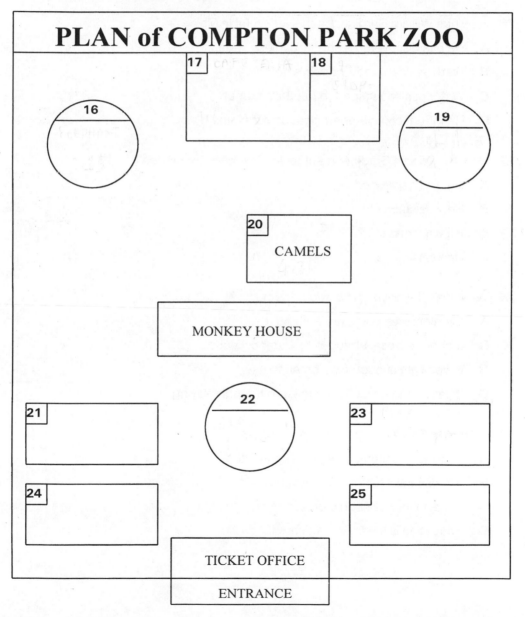

PLAN of COMPTON PARK ZOO

17		18

16

19

20

CAMELS

MONKEY HOUSE

22

21

23

24

25

TICKET OFFICE

ENTRANCE

PART FOUR

You will hear an excerpt from a radio programme called 'Your World'. William Gardiner, who has just come back to Britain after working in Malawi, discusses his work among the people of Malawi with the programme presenter. For questions **26-29**, indicate which of the alternatives **A**, **B**, **C** or **D** is the most appropriate response.

(When transferring your answers, write A, B, C or D on the answer sheet.)

26 How has William Gardiner been successful in Malawi?

    A   He has discovered a supply of clean water.

    B   Water is now nearer people's homes.

    C   Water has been piped to people's homes.

    D   He introduced water purification schemes.

A	
B	
C	
D	

27 How did William Gardiner react to what he calls 'ignorance'?

    A   He was depressed.

    B   He was scornful.

    C   He was frustrated.

    D   He was furious.

A	
B	
C	
D	

28 What was the clever thing about the pump?

    A   Even children could understand it.

    B   It changed local attitudes to water collection.

    C   It was light enough for women to use.

    D   It gave children a chance to learn through playing.

A	
B	
C	
D	

29 What was Gardiner's general conclusion?

    A   Expensive schemes are not appreciated.

    B   It is essential to get local support.

    C   Local initiatives should be exploited.

    D   Education is the first requirement.

A	
B	
C	
D	

PAPER 5 SPEAKING TEST   (about 15 minutes)

You will be asked to take part in a conversation with a group of other students or with your teacher. The conversation will be based on one particular topic area or theme, for example education, problems in society, the arts.

Of course each Speaking Test will be different for each student or group of students, but a *typical* test is described below.

★ At the start of the Speaking Test you will be asked to talk about one of the photographs among the Exercises on pages 117–119 at the back of the book; more than simple descriptions will be required.

★ You will then be asked to discuss one of the passages at the back of the book. Your teacher may ask you to talk about its content, where you think it comes from, who the author or speaker is, whether you agree or disagree with it, and so on. You will *not* be asked to read the passage aloud, but you may quote parts of it to make your point.

★ You may then be asked to discuss, for example, an advertisement, a leaflet, an extract from a newspaper, a quotation, etc. Your teacher will tell you which of the Speaking Test Exercises to look at.

★ You may also be asked to take part in an activity with a group of other students or your teacher which is intended to test your ability to interact successfully with other speakers during conversation and discussion in English. Your teacher will tell you which section among the Speaking Test Exercises you should look at.

Practice Test 3

PAPER 1 READING COMPREHENSION (1 hour)

There are **forty** questions on this paper. Attempt **all** questions. For each question there are four possible answers labelled **A, B, C** and **D**. Choose the **one** you consider correct and record your choice in **soft pencil** on the separate answer sheet.

Section A

In this section you must choose the word or phrase which best completes each sentence. **On your answer sheet**, indicate the letter **A, B, C** or **D** against the number of each item **1** to **25** for the word or phrase you choose. Give **one answer only** to each question.

1 The police were baffled by the attack as there seemed to be no apparent
   ....
   A design   **B** principle   **C** motive   **D** plot

2 If you want to be sure of receiving a copy of the magazine, I suggest you
   .... an annual subscription.
   A put down   **B** take out   **C** write off   **D** send up

3 After feeling off .... for days, Tom finally went to see his doctor.
   A food   **B** colour   **C** fitness   **D** balance

4 .... the phone rang later that night did Anna remember the appointment.
   A No sooner   **B** Only   **C** Not until   **D** Just before

5 There was .... evidence to bring charges against the man.
   A insubstantial   **B** inferior   **C** ineffective   **D** insufficient

6 The runner got a huge blister on his heel where his new shoes ....
   A scratched   **B** rubbed   **C** scraped   **D** gripped

7 The interviewer told Alison that she would earn £30,000 a year, ... she
   to be offered the job.
   A were   **B** should   **C** lest   **D** would

8 I .... to think what will happen if I turn up late again.
   A fear   **B** loathe   **C** despair   **D** dread

9 The Meteorological Office reported 20 centimetres of rain in October this year
   .... only 14 last year.
   A in comparison   **B** as against   **C** in contrast   **D** contrary to

10 The official inquiry into the accident .... the captain of all responsibility.
   A freed   **B** released   **C** cleared   **D** relinquished

11 It was with a .... heart that she said goodbye to all her colleagues.
   A solemn   **B** heavy   **C** dismal   **D** grim

12 Beatrice's mother .... her against taking too much luggage on her trip.
   A recommended   **B** encouraged   **C** reprimanded   **D** warned

13 Suddenly the room seemed to spin, my hands started shaking and I ....
   to the floor.
   A sank   **B** swayed   **C** passed   **D** fainted

14 Martin didn't .... the prospect of telling his father that he had spent all
   the money.
   A rejoice   **B** envy   **C** relish   **D** desire

15 The teacher obviously didn't like me because she was always .... on
   me.
   A setting   **B** picking   **C** keeping   **D** getting

16 I don't .... about the expense as long as you solve the problem.
   A object   **B** care   **C** argue   **D** complain

17 The boss .... into a rage and started shouting at Robert to do as he was
   told.
   A flew   **B** charged   **C** rushed   **D** burst

18 Unfortunately there now seems to be no .... to prevent the spread of
   these malicious rumours.
   A likelihood   **B** hope   **C** liability   **D** way

19 The consultant called in by the firm brought a ....A........... of experience to bear
   on the problem.
   A wealth   **B** realm   **C** bank   **D** hoard

20 They wandered around in circles for an hour before finally admitting they were
   well and .... lost.
   A completely   **B** thoroughly   **C** truly   **D** utterly

21 Politicians should never lose .... of the needs of the people they represent.
   A view   **B** sight   **C** regard   **D** prospect

22 The confidence trickster .... the old lady out of her life savings.
   A swindled   **B** robbed   **C** deceived   **D** misled

23 Jessica's hopes were .... when she wasn't selected for the team.
   A lowered   **B** smashed   **C** dashed   **D** dimmed

24 Michael put his mistake .... to lack of concentration.
   A down   **B** over   **C** through   **D** up

25 The club took the unprecedented .... of dropping their star player before the big match.
   A move   **B** tread   **C** step   **D** stride

Section B

In this section you will find after each of the passages a number of questions or unfinished statements about the passage, each with four suggested answers or ways of finishing. You must choose the one which you think fits best. **On your answer sheet**, indicate the letter **A, B, C** or **D** against the number of each item **26** to **40** for the answer you choose. Give **one answer only** to each question.

FIRST PASSAGE

The history of ancient Egypt would undoubtedly have remained largely unknown had Egyptologists been unable to penetrate the secrets of the hieroglyphic writing that covers countless monuments in the Nile delta. This style of writing, in contrast to cuneiform writing, which appears rather austere, geometric and abstract, is poetic, fascinating – indeed, almost alive – because it is created from beautifully stylised drawings: human heads, birds, a variety of animals, plants and flowers. The word 'hieroglyph', which refers to the characters used in the writing of the ancient Egyptians, means 'writing of the gods'. The earliest hieroglyphic inscriptions date back to the third millennium BC, but the script must have originated well before that. It underwent no major changes until AD 390, when Egypt was under the power of the Romans, although over the centuries the number of signs increased from approximately seven hundred to around five thousand. Whereas the early inscriptions of Mesopotamia only gradually developed from a form of aide-mémoire into a flexible writing system, the hieroglyphic system was from the beginning a true form of writing: first, because it could almost completely record the spoken language; and second, due to its ability to deal with abstract as well as concrete entities and to transcribe equally well texts concerning agriculture, medicine, law and education, religious prayers, traditional stories, and, indeed, literature in all its forms.

The originality and complexity of this writing system are largely due to the fact that in the main it is made up of three kinds of sign: pictograms – stylised drawings representing objects or beings, with combinations of the same signs to express ideas; phonograms – the same or different forms used to represent sounds; and finally determinatives – signs used to indicate which category of object or being is in question. This graphic system, a specific style of writing, was truly 'the writing of the gods'. Generally, divine names and those of the pharaohs, who were seen as gods, appear in the texts enclosed within a special shape called a 'cartouche', so that the sacred character of these words is immediately recognisable.

Most commonly, lines of hieroglyphs were written to be read from left to right. And this direction signalled the direction of the human and birds' heads; the person reading was intended to move his eyes in the same way. In practice, it was not always that simple. For example, if an inscription on the wall of a monument or temple were located near the statue of an important god or of a pharaoh, the faces in the inscription would be turned towards the statue, thus seemingly changing the direction of reading and making the text more difficult to understand. Hieroglyphs could also be written from bottom to top or in alternating directions: right to left on one line and then left to right on the following line.

Hieroglyphs are universally fascinating. The countless deities of ancient Egypt are glorified in hieroglyphs covering temple walls and tombs. It is almost as if the hieroglyphs themselves were sacred. These signs, whether engraved in stone or painted, have a beauty surpassing the merely human, and seem, irrespective of what is actually written, to be pure visual poems. In the eyes of the ancient Egyptians, they could only be of divine inspiration. And for us too, contemplating these wonders, they produce an effect akin to great poetry.

26 What was required before the history of ancient Egypt could be known?
   A the analysis of documents from the Nile delta
   B the deciphering of cuneiform writing
   C the classifying of drawings in varied styles
   D the interpretation of hieroglyphic writing

27 What advantage did early hieroglyphic writing have over inscriptions from Mesopotamia?
   A It allowed the recording of a range of subjects.
   B It was useful for the transmission of messages.
   C It fulfilled aesthetic needs.
   D It was simple to memorise.

28 How were abstract concepts conveyed by hieroglyphs?
    A by representing the sound of the word
    B by bringing together signs for ordinary objects
    C by using a special set of symbols
    D by enclosing signs in special shapes

29 In practice, how were lines of hieroglyphs meant to be read?
    A up one line and down the next
    B in the direction the heads were facing
    C left on one line and right on another
    D in a direction determined by key markers

30 What effect do hieroglyphics have on the writer?
    A He finds them challenging to decipher.
    B He is struck by the variety of symbolic forms.
    C He is filled with a feeling of awe.
    D He is perplexed by the great number of signs.

SECOND PASSAGE

It was the Scott family, with their polite codes of behaviour and their nice social distinctions, that set the tone for Paul's childhood. His mother, who came from south London, enthusiastically endorsed the outlook and values that went with her husband's sort of person. Frances Scott was a woman of powerful poetic imagination and driving will. All her life she consoled herself for reality's shortcomings with rich and extravagant dreams. She had written unpublished novels herself as a girl, working in a cupboard by candlelight. The night before her wedding in 1916 she said she read them all through and burned them. Her elder son, Peter, who was two years older than Paul, took after no-one in particular. But Paul had her own strong, distinctive family nose, and with it she passed on her creative energy and a burning sense of what he might do in the future. He had been a ten months' baby: she said she had carried him an extra month in the womb to allow time for his remarkable brain to develop. She had resented her pregnancy and had in any case hoped for a girl. But Paul was a prodigy in her eyes from birth. He walked and talked before he was one, and, according to his mother, who could never have enough of his achievements, he came pretty close to writing his first poem too. She had unheard-of ambitions for him; he grew up under the spell of his mother's imagination, and the spur of her great expectation. He was to fulfil her promise, redeem the hopes of her girlhood, make good the disappointments of a life that had never quite come up to scratch.

    Paul always insisted that he had a perfectly ordinary childhood, comfortable, happy and protected. He and his brother were the only children in a family heavily weighted towards the other end of the age scale. Their father had himself been the only boy in a household of women, petted and made much of by six sisters, none of whom ever married. Peter and Paul grew up in a circle of elderly maiden aunts, and Paul in particular energetically returned their interest. He was an enchanting infant, comical, astute and precocious. His sayings were treasured, his doings marvelled over, his jokes passed round the whole family. He seems to have been, even as a very small child, sharply aware of other people and unusually receptive. The earliest symptom he diagnosed in himself as a writer was an intense curiosity: he said it could prove dangerous later, but in childhood it meant that he gave as much as he got from the fond, admiring female relations bending over his cot.

All his life he remained an exceptional listener. People to whom he gave his full attention agree that there was nothing to match it. He listened with a sympathetic concentration that was irresistible, and the first voice he listened to was his mother's. He must have heard her building dream-castles for him to inhabit almost before he could understand what she was saying; and as soon as he could stagger to his feet, he brought her offerings in return – a toy boat with a bead in the bottom or a ring case with a coin lodged in its slot. Already he knew how to please her, and perhaps already he could hear, beneath her challenging, confident voice, another message, equally insistent but harsher and more plaintive. Paul's mother seldom talked about her past, except sometimes to recolour and recast it in a more satisfactory form. How much she told Paul, and how much he guessed, is impossible to say. But there can be no doubt that, for all the bold front she put on in public, Frances Scott was the forerunner of a line of lonely, vulnerable, insecure wives in his books, women whose energies found no outlet and whose talents ran slowly to waste.

31 When Frances married into the Scott family, she
  A considered them limited in their views.
  B resented the restrictions imposed on her.
  C was happy to accept their standards.
  D was pleased at their reaction to her talent.

32 As a married woman, how did Frances Scott come to terms with the realities of life?
  A She retreated into her imagination.
  B She indulged in fantasies about her social status.
  C She drove her children to succeed.
  D She developed her literary talents.

33 Being pregnant for the second time seemed to make Frances
  A formulate unrealistic plans.
  B want to spend time with Peter.
  C worry about Peter's reaction.
  D wish her family had been limited to one child.

34 When Paul was a young child, his mother
   A thought he was handsome.
   B exaggerated his abilities.
   C encouraged his literary gifts.
   D concealed her disappointment at having another son.

35 What was Paul's reaction to the attention he received from his aunts?
   A He would have preferred to have been left alone.
   B He treated it with indifference.
   C He responded enthusiastically.
   D He wished he received as much as his brother.

36 What aspect of his mother's experience later influenced Paul's writing?
   A the urge to invent stories
   B the need to develop strength of character
   C the ability to play a particular role in public
   D the frustration that comes with undeveloped talents

THIRD PASSAGE

When it comes to explaining complicated ideas, it is certainly not the case that the most efficient researcher is always the best communicator – although the best are frequently the most enthusiastic and are clearly deeply in love with their subject. Enthusiasm is regarded by some as a suspect, emotional involvement with no place in an academic environment. But it is a simple fact that genuine enthusiasm is highly infectious and is one of the most easily caught of communicable diseases. Undisguised love of the subject does more to bring fresh minds into science than all the text-books ever written and, once that spark of life has been lit, students go away and teach themselves.

The vast majority of practitioners of any art or science seem to construct a barrier around themselves lest others should steal the trick. In the sciences this takes the form of a carefully constructed and standardised nomenclature which is supposed to be a short-hand way of addressing complicated concepts and avoiding confusion. This generally works well but sometimes achieves just the opposite. The short-hand becomes a sort of pretentious verbal diarrhoea, intended to impress the uninitiated, demonstrate how adept the operator is, and build a barrier between the practitioner and the common man. There is clearly room for this sort of professional jargon in the research laboratory, but it is not the appropriate medium for popular or introductory instruction. This is a plea for the use of everyday English and common sense.

The folk who are involved in pushing back the frontiers are often the only ones who can explain their work to the intelligent public. They are forced to accept the role of interpreter in spreading news of advances to the people who actually pay for them, but they are often reluctant or ill-equipped to undertake this role. There is clearly the need for professional interpreters who are equally at home on both sides of the fence. Such intermediaries are rare and are more necessary today than ever before.

The unbelievably arrogant attitude of what is often regarded as 'descending to the level of the public' is merely an excuse for laziness. It may be difficult, irksome and tedious to rephrase one's ideas, without distorting them, but the effort can be rewarding. Anyone who has worked in a complicated and involved area of research knows how difficult it is to explain one's thoughts to interested laymen. But there is a hidden benefit. One soon realises that it is the best way of detecting errors in arguments and faults in theories before they are given premature publicity. It is also a fact that the fresh approach offered by a sympathetic listener can often bring out an error of interpretation which could become an embarrassing stumbling block later.

We need better communicators to catch the attention of fresh young minds and to present the advances of modern research in a digestible form. We do not need self-important egos that hide behind terminological barriers – we need the humility of the true amateur whose transparent enthusiasm can stimulate and influence while using the vocabulary of common sense. Surely this is what makes science such an attractive and living pursuit. All of us can learn from each other if we are prepared both to listen and to take the trouble to explain our own beliefs and prejudices.

37 What is the writer's view of enthusiasts?
   A They make the best researchers.
   B They are unlikely to communicate well.
   C They are a threat to the subjects they love.
   D They are important to the future development of their subjects.

38 What paradox surrounds the adoption of a standardised nomenclature in the sciences?
   A It is intended to be impressive.
   B It can make communication impossible.
   C Experts like to show off.
   D Ordinary people are unwilling to learn scientific terms.

39 What is the writer's view of scientific jargon?
   A It can be useful in its place.
   B It should be avoided at all costs.
   C It is beyond the competence of ordinary people.
   D It can lead to inaccuracy.

40 Those who make exciting scientific discoveries should be
   A allowed to work in privacy.
   B conscious of their responsibility to society.
   C involved in training presenters.
   D shown tolerance by the general public.

PAPER 2 COMPOSITION   (2 hours)

Answer any **two** questions.
Your answers must follow exactly the instructions given.
Write your answers on the separate answer paper provided.
Write clearly in pen, not pencil. You may make alterations but make sure that your work is **easy to read.** Write both question numbers clearly in the left-hand margin at the beginning of your answers.

1   Describe the job which you would most like to do and explain what appeals to you about it. (About 350 words)

2   It is said that some entertainment and sports personalities are paid far too much. What are your views on this? (About 350 words)

3   Write a short story beginning or ending with the words: *Chris closed the door thoughtfully. How good it was to be alone again.* (About 350 words)

4   You are organising an event to raise money for a worthwhile cause. Write a letter to your local newspaper giving details of the event and explaining how the money will be used. (About 300 words)

5   Based on your reading of **one** of these books, write on **one** of the following. (About 350 words)

HARPER LEE: *To Kill a Mocking Bird*
Describe how the relationship between Atticus and his children is influenced by certain important incidents in the story.

TIMOTHY MO: *Sour Sweet*
The Chinese characters in the novel make many observations on English habits and culture, some humorous, some not. Describe some of these and also some of the habits and culture of the Chinese themselves as revealed in the novel.

WILLIAM GOLDING: *Lord of the Flies*
Two symbols in the novel are the conch and the pig's head. Explain how they influence the story and what they represent.

PAPER 3 USE OF ENGLISH   (2 hours)

Section A

1   Fill each of the numbered blanks in the passage with **one** suitable word.

The concept of time

Astronomy was one of the earliest of the sciences. Primitive man saw the sun
rising **(1)** .... different times, but always on the **(2)** ....
horizon. He saw it set, but always on the *opposite* horizon, and so he
recognised the rising in the east and the **(3)** .... in the west. Given
(4) .... fixed point of reference – a pillar, a tree or a pole – he
noticed that the shadows that moved **(5)** .... it were longer in the
morning and evening, and at their **(6)** .... when the sun was highest
in the sky at noon. He acquired a sense of timekeeping **(7)** .... the
shortest shadow conveniently divided his working day **(8)** ....
morning and afternoon, **(9)** .... the heat of the noonday sun to
emphasise this **(10)** .... Thousands of years ago,
(11) .... astronomy was in **(12)** .... infancy, it was
realised that the movements of the stars followed a consistent pattern, in
(13) .... groups of stars appeared to change **(14)** ....
positions as the night progressed, just **(15)** .... the sun did during
the day. In the Northern Hemisphere the observer **(16)** .... notice
that **(17)** .... star (the Pole Star) would always be seen
(18) .... the same point on the horizon at sunrise and sunset,
(19) .... the other stars revolved about the fixed star from east to

west. So, **(20)** .... the 'shadow clock' of the daytime he added the 'star clock' of the night.

2   Finish each of the following sentences in such a way that it is **as similar as possible in meaning to the sentence printed before it.**

EXAMPLE: I expect that he will get there by lunchtime.

ANSWER: I expect him *to get there by lunchtime.*

a)   If his solicitor hadn't advised him, he would have made a serious mistake.

Had it ....

....

b)   He would never agree to sell his business, even if he received a very tempting offer.

However ....

....

c)   Something must be done quickly to solve the problem of homelessness.

Urgent ....

....

d)   You could be arrested for not giving a breath sample to the police.

Refusal ....

....

e)   Philip's inability to make decisions dates from his accident.

Ever ....

....

f)   I really like her voice but not her choice of songs.

Much ....

....

g)   He delayed writing the book until he had done a lot of research.

Only ....

....

h) Don't go to lunch until you have typed all these letters.

Make sure you finish ....

....

3 Fill each of the blanks with a suitable word or phrase.

EXAMPLE: He doesn't mind one way or the other; it makes *no difference to* him.

a) I rang the police though I wasn't sure .... to do or not.

b) I'm moving in June but .... being I'll be at this address.

c) Whatever faults John may have, meanness .... of them.

d) If you don't phone Sam before 5.30 pm he .... the office and gone home.

e) Finding nothing in the fridge, I .... but to go out to eat.

f) Terence is far .... invested all his money in one company.

4 For each of the sentences below, write a new sentence **as similar as possible in meaning to the original sentence**, but using the word given. This word **must not be altered in any way.**

EXAMPLE: Not many people attended the meeting.
turnout

ANSWER: *There was a poor turnout for the meeting.*

a) I owe three weeks' rent.
behind

....

b) These two makes of computer are practically the same.
hardly

....

....

c) Who will inherit the estate?
heir

....

d) The bottle must not be laid on its side.
upright

....

e) The manager told his staff that he was pleased, but they could do better.
room

....

....

f) Salaries have doubled in the last ten years.
twice

....

....

g) What you have been saying is quite irrelevant.
beside

....

....

h) He likes to be addressed as 'Professor'.
call

....

....

Section B

5   Read this passage, then answer the questions which follow it.

Escape routes

Our existence is mapped by a life plan. Ahead of us run the career lines of our jobs, our marriage, our leisure interests, our children and our economic fortunes. But sometimes when we scan these maps, traverse these routes, follow the signs, we become strangely disturbed by the predictability of the journey, the accuracy of the map, the knowledge that   5
today's route will be much like yesterday's. The route we take to work, the clothes we wear, the food we eat, are visible reminders of an awful sense of monotony.

For some people, such feelings may be so intense that they are led to search for alternative realities; they set out to change their whole world.   10
But most of us do not wish to rid ourselves of these involvements altogether. What we object to is the sense that we are sinking into a patterned way of existence in all these areas; that they no longer appear to us as fresh and novel. They are becoming routine. They no longer help us to constitute our identity.   15

When we ourselves begin to perceive our own life as stretching out in this patterned way, we may question its meaning. The regularised nature of our life begins to loom within consciousness as a cause for dissatisfaction, as a reason why we feel that something must be done about it. We therefore have to work hard to dispel the apparent ways in   20
which our sense of individuality is being threatened. We have to retain a vision of ourselves as only partially determined creatures.

One way is to reflect that although much of our life certainly does look like a series of sequences through which we pass, nevertheless these are adequately balanced by those areas of freedom and spontaneity that we   25
have constructed for ourselves. To feel that many aspects of our existence are routine is tolerable as long as they do not usurp such free domains. We rationalise our way of life by declaring that the ideal state is some equilibrium between the routine and indeterminate aspects of our existence. Unless the correct balance is achieved, unhappiness will result.   30

But though our occasional restlessness about the extent of habit in our life may be temporarily banished by recourse to some such theory of human happiness, it may return as we reflect upon the sheer predictability of our lives. However much we revolve domestic, occupational and leisure images, we still come up with patterned pictures. As in a   35
kaleidoscope, the colours change, but the symmetry persists. Our relationship with our relatives seems indistinguishable from those paraded in the soap operas of radio and television. We appear to live by order, moving from gramophone to stereo system, from refrigerator to

deep freeze, along the market tramlines of consumer society. How may we declare ourselves still free, individual and unique, when uniformity asserts itself so massively within our daily life?

There is a solution; we can not only accept this increase in uniformity as real, but proclaim it as a pre-condition for freedom. Far from encroaching upon freedom, habit makes room for it. The more we are able to view inessential elements of our life as unreflective chains of behaviour, the more we can concentrate upon self-expression in the remaining areas. We can allow the advertisers to stock our cupboards and kitchens and garages, we can happily buy mass-produced clothes off the peg and become lost in the anonymous ritualised journeys to and from work, for we know that this surrenders nothing that is important to ourselves. Our life and actions in these places seem artificial; real life is elsewhere. We may all look like uniform beings, but that is an illusion. Differentiation and diversity are occurring elsewhere.

a) In what ways can our life plan make us feel uneasy?

....

....

b) What do a minority of people do in response to their life plan?

....

....

c) What do most people feel is lost as a result of routine?

....

....

d) What is meant in this context by the phrase 'begins to loom within consciousness'? (line 18)

....

....

e) According to the writer, why is our 'sense of individuality' (line 21) not under serious threat?

....

....

f) What can help us to compensate for the sequential nature of life?

....

....

g) What, according to the writer, is the way to avoid unhappiness?

....

....

h) What phrase is used by the writer to convey the idea that 'our occasional restlessness' (line 31) may return?

....

....

i) Explain the implications of 'moving from gramophone to stereo system, from refrigerator to deep freeze'. (lines 39-40)

....

....

j) According to the last paragraph, why might habit be viewed in a positive light?

....

....

k) In your own words, give **two** examples of uniform behaviour from the last paragraph.

....

....

l) In a paragraph of 60-80 words, summarise the ways in which human beings may react to the monotony of routine.

....

....

....

....

....

....

....

....

....

....

....

....

PAPER 4 LISTENING COMPREHENSION (about 35 minutes)

In the live examination, you will have to transfer your answers to the separate answer sheet. See page 134 for a sample answer sheet.

PART ONE

You will hear part of a radio programme in which a woman is interviewed about her success. For questions **1-5**, indicate which of the alternatives **A, B, C** or **D** is the most appropriate response.

(When transferring your answers, write A, B, C or D on the answer sheet.)

1 Which of these is Pamela's main asset?

A	instinct
B	youth
C	energy
D	background

A	
B	
C	
D	

2 What did Pamela's teachers think about her future?

A	She would only be good at typing.
B	She would be quite unsuited to any kind of work.
C	She would only be suited to a low grade job.
D	She would be good at jobs requiring quick decisions.

A	
B	
C	
D	

3 How does Pamela account for her exceptional professional success?

A	She has a better intuition than men.
B	She can make effective decisions quickly.
C	She has a relaxed attitude at times of crisis.
D	She knows her subject thoroughly.

A	
B	
C	
D	

4 How does she think some listeners will regard her view on animal rights?

A that poverty is a more important issue	A
B that she is being trivial	B
C that she is too interested in fashion	C
D that she is inconsistent	D

5 What would she like to do in the future?

A develop a more active social conscience	A
B continue in her current job	B
C work and simultaneously help other people	C
D give up her present job and help poorer people	D

PART TWO

You will hear the introduction to a public talk, and part of the talk itself, given by a woman called Tina Wilson who has problems with her hearing and sight. For questions **6-13**, complete the notes made by a member of the audience with a word or a short phrase.

(When transferring your answers, write the word or short phrase, as appropriate, on the answer sheet.)

Hearing
What use are Tina's hearing aids?

INDOORS: she can   **6**

OUTDOORS: she can   **7**

            she can't   **8**

Sight
How good is her eyesight?

PERIPHERAL VISION: **9**

CENTRAL VISION: **10**

Why is her use of a cane limited?   **11**

Transport
What problems does she have with public transport?

BUS: worst problem is   **12**

UNDERGROUND: worst problem is   **13**

PART THREE

You will hear part of a radio interview in which an author talks about his recent book, and a psychologist is asked to comment. For questions **14-19**, indicate which of the alternatives **A, B, C** or **D** is the most appropriate response.

(When transferring your answers, write A, B, C or D on the answer sheet.)

14 By removing his uniform the officer

    A   lost his life.

    B   caused the battle to be lost.

    C   was expelled from the regiment.

    D   lost respect.

A	
B	
C	
D	

15 Richard is wearing a suit

    A   instead of a uniform.

    B   to be part of a group.

    C   because he likes suits.

    D   because it is a rule.

A	
B	
C	
D	

16 What is said about prisoners in camps?

    A   They secretly tried on their captors' clothes.

    B   They spent the little money they had on uniforms.

    C   They tried to make clothes like those of the guards.

    D   They were punished for not wearing uniforms.

A	
B	
C	
D	

17 Why did Richard feel different at school?

    A   He was too busy studying.

    B   Because he had to wear a uniform.

    C   Because he wasn't good at sport.

    D   Because of his religion.

A	
B	
C	
D	

18 What does the psychologist imply about people who campaign against pornography?

- **A** They are socially unacceptable.
- **B** They are hypocritical.
- **C** They are public spirited.
- **D** They are highly moral.

A	
B	
C	
D	

19 What is Richard's attitude to uniform?

- **A** condemnation
- **B** reluctant approval
- **C** scornful
- **D** dislike mixed with fascination

A	
B	
C	
D	

PART FOUR

You will hear an interview about the effects of high levels of noise in discotheques on people's hearing. For questions **20-29**, indicate the correct response by circling TRUE or FALSE.

(When transferring your answers, write T or F on the answer sheet.)

20 Peter Johnson is a Mental Health Officer.   TRUE/FALSE

21 He says he has no figures on disco attendance.   TRUE/FALSE

22 If you attend loud discos often, your ears get used to the noise.   TRUE/FALSE

23 Study of this problem at Southampton is comparatively new.   TRUE/FALSE

24 Too much disco noise like this causes complete loss of hearing.   TRUE/FALSE

25 4,000 personal stereos were sold in 1982.   TRUE/FALSE

26 John Bickerdyke is a lecturer at Southampton University.   TRUE/FALSE

27 The noise levels of personal stereos can be the same as some factory machines.   TRUE/FALSE

28 Johnson thinks Bickerdyke's proposals should be generally adopted.   TRUE/FALSE

29 He says protecting people from excessive noise should be the responsibility of disco managers.   TRUE/FALSE

PAPER 5 SPEAKING TEST   (about 15 minutes)

You will be asked to take part in a conversation with a group of other students or with your teacher. The conversation will be based on one particular topic area or theme, for example education, problems in society, the arts.

Of course each Speaking Test will be different for each student or group of students, but a *typical* test is described below.

★ At the start of the Speaking Test you will be asked to talk about one of the photographs among the Exercises on pages 120–122 at the back of the book; more than simple descriptions will be required.

★ You will then be asked to discuss one of the passages at the back of the book. Your teacher may ask you to talk about its content, where you think it comes from, who the author or speaker is, whether you agree or disagree with it, and so on. You will *not* be asked to read the passage aloud, but you may quote parts of it to make your point.

★ You may then be asked to discuss, for example, an advertisement, a leaflet, an extract from a newspaper, a quotation, etc. Your teacher will tell you which of the Speaking Test Exercises to look at.

★ You may also be asked to take part in an activity with a group of other students or your teacher which is intended to test your ability to interact successfully with other speakers during conversation and discussion in English. Your teacher will tell you which section among the Speaking Test Exercises you should look at.

Practice Test 4

PAPER 1 READING COMPREHENSION (1 hour)

There are **forty** questions on this paper. Attempt **all** questions. For each question there are four possible answers labelled **A**, **B**, **C** and **D**. Choose the **one** you consider correct and record your choice in **soft pencil** on the separate answer sheet.

Section A

In this section you must choose the word or phrase which best completes each sentence. **On your answer sheet**, indicate the letter **A**, **B**, **C** or **D** against the number of each item **1** to **25** for the word or phrase you choose. Give **one answer only** to each question.

1 In the .... of security, personnel must wear their identity badges at all times.
   A requirement   **B** interests   **C** demands   **D** assistance

2 The strike was .... owing to a last-minute agreement with the management.
   A called off   **B** broken up   **C** set back   **D** put down

3 Lindsay's excuses for being late are beginning to .... rather thin.
   A get   **B** turn   **C** wear   **D** go

4 ...., the people who come to this club are in their twenties and thirties.
   A By and large   **B** Altogether   **C** To a degree   **D** Virtually

5 My cousin was nervous about being interviewed on television, but she rose to the .... wonderfully.
   A event   **B** performance   **C** incident   **D** occasion

6 The train service has been a .... since they introduced the new schedules.
   A shambles   **B** rumpus   **C** chaos   **D** fracas

7 Is an inexperienced civil servant .... to the task of running the company?
   A capable   **B** skilled   **C** eligible   **D** suited

8 John's got very .... feelings about taking on more responsibility at the moment.
A puzzled   **B** jumbled   **C** mixed   **D** muddled

9 You've lived in the city for most of your life, so .... you're used to the noise.
A apparently   **B** presumably   **C** allegedly   **D** predictably

10 The storm ripped our tent to ....
A slices   **B** shreds   **C** strips   **D** specks

11 His heartless treatment of his former colleague revealed a .... of cruelty in his nature.
A taint   **B** stain   **C** mark   **D** streak

12 The deceptively simple decoration on this kind of pottery gives the layperson no real .... to its true value.
A idea   **B** indication   **C** clue   **D** key

13 The winter is usually mild, although we sometimes get a cold .... at the beginning of the year.
A spell   **B** term   **C** interval   **D** wave

14 Although the council had expected opposition to the scheme, the local residents proved only too .... to help.
A anxious   **B** concerned   **C** hasty   **D** cautious

15 The newspaper had been tipped .... about the star's arrival and sent a photographer to the airport.
A up   **B** in   **C** off   **D** on

16 The new school timetable will .... rearranging the meal breaks.
A incur   **B** need   **C** oblige   **D** mean

17 Can I .... your brains for a moment? I can't do this crossword by myself.
A have   **B** pick   **C** mind   **D** use

18 Rosemary .... Chris to buy a new car with the proceeds of the sale.
A pressed   **B** insisted   **C** offered   **D** afforded

19 There was an open day at the fire .... when the public could see how the fire brigade operated.
A centre   **B** station   **C** offices   **D** quarters

20 .... what most people say about him, he has a very good sense of humour.

    A Opposite to   **B** Against   **C** Contrary to   **D** Opposing

21 All those late nights must be .... their toll because Becky looks quite exhausted.

    A taking   **B** having   **C** holding   **D** keeping

22 It was the brilliant forensic work of the pathologist that eventually .... to the arrest of the criminal.

    A produced   **B** resulted   **C** brought   **D** led

23 Stephanie is at her desk from dawn till dusk and seems to .... on working hard.

    A flourish   **B** succeed   **C** thrive   **D** prosper

24 If I make a fool of myself in front of my friends, I'll never .... it down.

    A let   **B** give   **C** settle   **D** live

25 You haven't heard all the facts so don't .... to conclusions.

    A dash   **B** jump   **C** spring   **D** fly

Section B

In this section you will find after each of the passages a number of questions or unfinished statements about the passage, each with four suggested answers or ways of finishing. You must choose the one which you think fits best. **On your answer sheet**, indicate the letter **A**, **B**, **C** or **D** against the number of each item **26** to **40** for the answer you choose. Give **one answer only** to each question.

FIRST PASSAGE

The assertion that mathematics has been a major force in the moulding of modern culture appears to many people incredible or, at best, a rank exaggeration. This disbelief results from a very common but erroneous conception of what mathematics really is. Influenced by what was taught in school, the average person regards mathematics as a series of techniques of use only to the scientist, the engineer and perhaps the financier. The reaction to such teaching is distaste for the subject and a decision to ignore it. When challenged on this decision, a well-read person can obtain the support of authorities. No less a personage than Schopenhauer, the philosopher, described mathematics as the lowest activity of the spirit, as is shown by the fact that it can be performed by a machine. Despite such authoritative judgements, the layman's decision to ignore mathematics is wrong. The subject is not a series of techniques. These are indeed the least important aspect. The techniques are mathematics stripped of motivation, reasoning, beauty and significance.

Let us consider the twentieth-century view of the subject. Primarily, mathematics is a method of inquiry known as postulational thinking. The method consists in carefully formulating definitions of the concepts to be discussed and in explicitly stating the assumptions that are the basis for reasoning. From these definitions and assumptions, conclusions are deduced by the application of the most rigorous logic man is capable of using. Mathematics is also a field of creative endeavour. In divining what can be proved, as well as in constructing methods of proof, mathematicians employ a high order of intuition and imagination. Kepler and Newton, for example, were men of wonderful imaginative powers, which enabled them not only to break away from age-long and rigid tradition but also to set up new and revolutionary concepts.

If mathematics is indeed a creative activity, what driving force causes men to pursue it? The most obvious motive has been to answer questions arising directly out of social needs. Commercial and financial transactions, navigation and calendar-reckoning involve problems that can best be resolved by mathematics. Another basic use of mathematics has been to provide a rational organisation of natural phenomena. The concepts, methods, and conclusions of mathematics are the substratum of the physical sciences. The success of these fields has been dependent on the extent to which they have entered into partnership with mathematics. Mathematics has brought life to the dry bones of disconnected facts and has bound various series of detached observations into bodies of science.

26 What happens when ordinary people are told that mathematics has played a major role in modern culture?
   A They express a dislike of the subject.
   B They claim the statement is false.
   C They are reluctant to accept this.
   D They dismiss mathematics as a series of techniques.

27 Why is Schopenhauer's assertion unacceptable?
   A It runs contrary to common experience.
   B His analysis of mathematics is too narrow.
   C It overestimates the power of machines.
   D Logic is required in solving problems.

28 Which of the following is characteristic of postulational thinking?
   A thinking in an inspirational manner
   B breaking away from established traditions
   C being explicit about the basis of reasoning
   D establishing what proofs are acceptable

29 What has been the dominant urge in the study of mathematics?
   A the need to tackle practical difficulties
   B the pursuit of abstract truths
   C the search for an explanation of physical reality
   D the desire to be creative

SECOND PASSAGE

It would be hard to argue that I followed Alicia Davie, exactly. Generally, yes, I do go directly home, but not always. I had a number of things to do on that side of the city. I caught up with her at the end of Junction Street. I came up on her right-hand side, slowed my brisk pace to hers, then disconcerted her by failing to speak and simply reaching out for the books she carried. Faltering, she let me take them from her. I turned them over as we walked, and peered at the lettering on the spines: Fitzhugh and Skidmont, Thomas Urquhart, Alasdair Mackie. She couldn't be working on anything for one of my courses at the university.

'I go down here.' She indicated the street that stretched off behind her. I gave it a brief glance over her shoulder: Ardmonry Road; drab, mean and very poorly lit.

'I'll walk you home.'

Stacking the lump of books out the way under one arm, I turned to Alicia and offered her the other. Since she made no move to take it, I reached out for one of her chilled hands and tucked it neatly under my elbow. Her arm relaxed a little in mine. She had already launched into the eternal all-purpose student bleat about her lodgings, how cold her room was and how expensive, how far from the bus stop, how mean the landlord was. By the time we had forced our way down the street together, arm in arm, in the teeth of a bitter wind as far as number eighteen, I had stopped listening to her entirely.

It looked a nasty little house, the sort of place I hadn't been in for years: that concrete path, almost too narrow to walk along in safety, leading past all those scruffy plants and that other thinner strip of concrete peeling away towards the side door. It was down this offshoot that Alicia Davie led me, stepping with all the confidence of familiarity along the rutted, ill-pitched pathway. Upstairs and down, none of the uncurtained windows was lamplit, but as my companion failed to remark on this, I took it for an indication that she was accustomed to returning at night to an empty house, and wondered, not for the first time, with whom she shared it. It looked a most unpleasant place to come home to.

You'd think I might have been prepared. But nothing can ever prepare one for the sheer horror of student squalor. It hits you in the face like a brick each time you see it. She flicked the light switch and there it all was. The vile, murk-coloured carpet and walls, the ill-matched sheets on the ill-made bed, the hideous posters of unshaven heroes and uncombed heroines. Books lay all over, faces down, covers akimbo, their spines weakened beyond redemption, a bibliophile's darkest nightmare. Her clothes were scattered all about, woollens draped over the radiator, outdoor clothes piled across the back of the chair. Nests of crumpled jeans lay in the corners, and panties and socks and tights were apparently breeding everywhere, quite indiscriminately, with one another. Papers littered the floor, the shelves, the bed, the desk. My poor heart sank. Perhaps she noticed I was looking a little bit off-colour, for in an impromptu eruption of civility she offered to make me a cup of tea.

'You're very kind but I had best be off.'

She might have been a little disappointed. She looked as if she might be. But just at that moment, what I had taken to be a fur lining on a jacket on the armchair began to stir and stretch and yawn its way into a sleek and stripy fattish cat, and any mild desire she may have had that I should stay was clean forgotten in the flurry of scooping up and stroking and rubbing and welcoming.

'I'll be away.'

She rose, the cat tucked in her arms.

'Goodnight then.'

As I stepped back into the dark of the garden and heard with relief the door close behind me, I made myself the firm and tranquillising promise that I would never, under any circumstances, venture down Ardmonry Road again.

30 What was Alicia's initial reaction to the writer's presence?
  A She was excited.
  B She was surprised.
  C She was frightened.
  D She was pleased.

31 As they walked along, Alicia
  A started talking about matters of mutual interest.
  B made an amusing remark.
  C complained about her accommodation.
  D invited him to her home.

32 What did the house suggest to the writer about its occupants?
  A They lived independent lives.
  B They co-ordinated their routines.
  C They studied at different institutions.
  D They liked spending time together.

33 How did the writer react to the sight of Alicia's room?
  A He was prepared for what he saw.
  B It was worse than he had expected.
  C The decoration surprised him.
  D He was overcome with nostalgia.

34 What was Alicia's attitude to books?
   A She chose them with care.
   B She allowed others in the house to use them.
   C She found them a necessary irritation.
   D She was indifferent to their physical condition.

35 Why did the writer think Alicia offered to make some tea?
   A She wanted to make him feel better.
   B She realised she had been rude.
   C She needed to ask him for advice.
   D She wanted him to stay longer.

THIRD PASSAGE

It seems to me unlikely that any important portraits will ever be painted again. Portraits, that is to say, in the sense of portraiture as we now understand it. I can imagine multi-medium memento-sets devoted to the character of particular individuals. But these will have nothing to do with the works now hanging in portrait galleries.

The beginning of the decline of the painted portrait coincided roughly speaking with the rise of photography. The photographer had taken the place of the portrait painter. Photography was more accurate, quicker and far cheaper; it offered the opportunity of portraiture to the whole of society whereas previously such an opportunity had been the privilege of a very small elite. To counter the logic of the argument, painters and their patrons invented a number of mysterious, metaphysical qualities with which to prove that what the painted portrait offered was incomparable. Only man, not a machine, could interpret the soul of a sitter. An artist dealt with the sitter's destiny; the camera with mere light and shade. An artist judged; a photographer recorded.

All this is doubly untrue. First, it denies the interpretative role of the photographer, which is considerable. Secondly, it claims for painted portraits a psychological insight which ninety-nine per cent of them totally lack. If one is considering portraiture as a genre, it is no good thinking of a few extraordinary pictures, but rather of the endless portraits of the local nobility and dignitaries in countless provincial museums and town halls. The comparatively few portraits that reveal true psychological insight suggest personal, obsessional interests on the part of the artist which simply cannot be accommodated within the professional role of the portrait painter. Ask yourself the following hypothetical question: suppose that there is somebody in the second half of the nineteenth century in whom you are interested but of whose face you have never seen a picture. Would you rather find a painting or a photograph of this person?

Until the invention of photography, the painted portrait was the principal means of recording and presenting the likeness of a person. Photography took over this role from painting and at the same time raised our standards for

PAPER 2 COMPOSITION (2 hours)

Answer any **two** questions.
Your answers must follow exactly the instructions given.
Write your answers on the separate answer paper provided.
Write clearly in pen, not pencil. You may make alterations but make sure that your work is **easy to read.** Write both question numbers clearly in the left-hand margin at the beginning of your answers.

1   Describe a person whom you have known well for a long time, showing how your perception of that person has changed with the passing of time. (About 350 words)

2   'The growth in the world's population is probably the biggest problem facing mankind today.' Discuss this statement and offer some possible solutions to this problem. (About 350 words)

3   Write a story entitled *The Last Chance*. (About 350 words)

4   Write a letter to your superior asking permission to be excused from work to take part in an important family occasion. You should give details of the event and indicate how your work can be re-organised during your absence. (About 300 words)

5   Based on your reading of **one** of these books, write on **one** of the following. (About 350 words)

    RUTH PRAWER JHABVALA: *Heat and Dust*
    How was Olivia influenced by the Nawab and what were the immediate and long-term effects?

    TIMOTHY MO: *Sour Sweet*
    Briefly describe the activities of the Wo society and show how these affect the lives of the Chen family.

    WILLIAM GOLDING: *Lord of the Flies*
    Compare the characters of Ralph and Piggy and describe how their relationship develops.

PAPER 3 USE OF ENGLISH   (2 hours)

Section A

1   Fill each of the numbered blanks in the passage with **one** suitable word.

Short-term memory

One of the most important results of research into ageing has been to pinpoint
the significance of short-term memory. This faculty **(1)** .... easily
disturbed as ageing advances. **(2)** .... seems to happen is that
(3) .... is received by the brain, which scans it for meaning in order
to decode it at some future **(4)** .... It looks as if the actual capacity
of the short-term memory itself may not change too much **(5)** ....
age. A young man and a man in his late fifties **(6)** .... both be able
to remember and repeat an average of eight numbers recited to
(7) .... But what does change is that **(8)** .... the older
man is asked to remember **(9)** .... else between the time he is first
given the numbers to memorise and the time he is **(10)** .... to
repeat them, he will be much **(11)** .... likely to remember the
original numbers than the young man. **(12)** .... is because the
scanning stage is more easily disrupted by other activities in
(13) .... people.

   In **(14)** .... living one experiences this as a fairly minor
(15) .... – a telephone number forgotten while one
(16) .... up an area code, or the first part of complicated street
directions **(17)** .... with the last because the last 'turn lefts' and

'turn rights' have interfered **(18)** .... remembering the first directions. In more formal learning, however, the decay of short-term memory is **(19)** .... than just a mild social embarrassment. It can be a serious bar to further **(20)** ...., or indeed to any progress at all.

2 Finish each of the following sentences in such a way that it is **as similar as possible in meaning to the sentence printed before it.**

EXAMPLE: Immediately after his arrival things went wrong.

ANSWER: No sooner *had he arrived than things went wrong.*

a) I shall never lend Robert any more money, no matter what happens.

Under no ....

....

b) We were very impressed by the new cinema but found it rather expensive.

Impressed ....

....

c) The doctor advised him against taking a holiday in a tropical country.

The doctor's ....

....

d) It's more than a fortnight since anyone saw Julian.

Julian was ....

....

e) The deadline for the receipt of completed application forms is 3.00 p.m. on Friday, 18th December.

Completed application forms must ....

....

f) My uncle's generosity enabled us to go on a Mediterranean cruise.

Thanks ....

....

g) We've been trying to sell our house for well over six months.

Our house ....

....

h) In order to make a profit the new leisure centre needs at least 2,000 visitors a month.

No fewer ....

....

3 Fill each of the blanks with a suitable word or phrase.

EXAMPLE: He doesn't mind one way or the other; it makes *no difference to* him.

a) Mike's mother agreed to .... a motorbike with his own money, as long as he took lessons.

b) We .... walk back if you hadn't had your car.

c) Never .... play, I can't say if Pete is good enough to be in the hockey team.

d) I .... bothered to do any more housework today. I'm worn out.

e) I really need to know .... not they'll be coming on Monday, so I'll give them a ring.

f) I was so amazed at his behaviour I .... word to say.

4 For each of the sentences below, write a new sentence **as similar as possible in meaning to the original sentence**, but using the word given. This word **must not be altered in any way.**

EXAMPLE: Not many people attended the meeting.
  turnout

ANSWER: *There was a poor turnout for the meeting.*

a) You cannot choose which hotel you stay at on this package holiday.
option

....

....

81

b) My impression of her is that she is a very effective teacher.
strikes

....

....

c) I don't feel like going to the party.
mood

....

....

d) I certainly won't change my mind about resigning.
question

....

....

e) He didn't mention our previous conversation at all.
reference

....

....

f) We run the business together.
joint

....

....

g) Digging the garden always makes me feel hungry.
gives

....

....

h) The music teacher was the only member of staff not to attend the farewell party.
exception

....

....

Section B

5 Read this passage, then answer the questions which follow it.

Sport and television in the 21st century

'I wish to subscribe for the final of the Football Championship which is being shown again this evening.' 'Fine, give me your personal code number.' A telephone, more likely, a computer conversation which is short and direct. This will be the way of the sports consumer in the first decades of the 21st century. 5

Sport is heading for an indissoluble marriage with television and the passive spectator, the voyeur of emotions and efforts by others, will enjoy a private paradise. All of this will be in the future of sport. The spectator (the television audience) will be the priority and professional clubs will have to readjust their structures to adapt to the new reality: sport as a 10 business.

The new technologies will mean that spectators will no longer have to wait for broadcasts by the conventional channels. They will be the ones who decide what to see. And they will have to pay for it. In the United States the system of the future has already started: pay-as-you-view. 15 Everything will be offered by television and the spectator will only have to choose. The review *Sports Illustrated* recently published a full profile of the life of the supporter at home in the middle of the next century. It explained that the consumers would be able to select their view of the match on a gigantic, flat screen occupying the whole of one wall, with 20 images of a clarity which cannot be foreseen at present; they could watch from the trainer's bench, from the stands just behind the batter in a game of baseball or from the helmet of the star player in an American football game. And at their disposal will be the same options the producer of the recorded programme has: to select replays, to choose which camera to 25 use and to decide on the sound – whether to hear the public, the players, the trainer and so on.

Many sports executives, largely too old and too conservative to feel at home with the new technologies, still believe that sport must control the expansion of television coverage in order to survive and ensure that 30 spectators attend matches. They do not even accept the evidence which contradicts their view: while there is more basketball than ever on television, for example, it is also certain that basketball is more popular than ever.

It is also the argument of these sports executives that television is 35 harming the modest teams. This is true, but the future of those teams is also modest. They have reached their ceiling. It is the law of the market. The great events continually attract larger audiences.

The world is being constructed on new technologies so that people can make the utmost use of their time and, in their home, have access to the greatest possible range of recreational activities. Sport will have to adapt itself to the new world. 40

The most visionary executives go further. Their philosophy is: rather than see television take over sport, why not have sport take over television? This is already the case in the US, where there are plans for the baseball, American football, basketball and ice hockey leagues to create their own television channels or share ownership in others. The events would be offered by the 35 leagues and the benefits would accrue to those sports. A spectator could pay $1 to see a major final. If the potential audience in the US is 30 million households, the organising league would receive $30 million for a single match. The leagues would benefit but so would the athletes, converted into artistes capable of drawing the greatest audiences in the world. 45 50

The path will be traumatic but this *will* be the future. The new generation will call for sport in the best conditions and as cheap as possible. 55

a)   What is implied by the phrase 'sports consumer'? (line 4)

....

....

b)   What does the writer mean by the use of the phrase 'an indissoluble marriage' in line 6?

....

....

c)   Why will professional clubs have to 'readjust their structures'? (line 10)

....

....

d)   Who are 'they' in line 14?

....

....

e)   What is meant by the word 'profile' in line 17?

....

....

f) Explain in your own words what many sports executives believe about the new technologies.

....

....

g) According to the writer, what does the future hold for 'modest teams'? (line 36)

....

....

h) What is meant by the word 'visionary' in line 43?

....

....

i) How can sport take over television?

....

....

j) Explain the phrase 'the benefits would accrue to those sports'. (lines 48-49)

....

....

k) In your own words, how will sportsmen and sportswomen benefit from the changes mentioned?

....

....

l) What, according to the writer, will be 'traumatic'? (line 54)

....

....

m) In a paragraph of 60-80 words, summarise the facilities which will be available to the television sports spectator in the 21st century, according to the passage.

....

....

....

....

....

....

....

....

....

....

....

PAPER 4 LISTENING COMPREHENSION (about 35 minutes)

In the live examination, you will have to transfer your answers to the separate answer sheet. See page 134 for a sample answer sheet.

PART ONE

You will hear an extract from a radio sports programme. It is about a sport called six-day racing. For questions **1-7**, complete the notes taken during the interview, with a number, a word or a short phrase.

(When transferring your answers, write the number, word or short phrase, as appropriate, on the answer sheet.)

SIX-DAY RACING

First became popular in late **[1]** ☐

George Littlewood's record of **[2]** ☐ miles broken by

Kouros in **[3]** ☐

[4] ☐ other athletes have broken this record.

ATHLETES

Name	Nationality	Notes
Max Courtillon	French	63. Spartathlon in 32 hrs 28 mins
James Zarei	**[5]** ☐	Spartathlon in 29 hrs 49 mins
Tirtha Phani	Indian	Hopes to achieve longest **[6]** ☐
David Cooper	British	won **[7]** ☐

PART TWO

You will hear an interview with a woman who allowed her house to be used as the location for a film. For questions **8-12,** indicate which of the alternatives **A**, **B**, **C** or **D** is the most appropriate response.

(When transferring your answers, write A, B, C or D on the answer sheet.)

8 As her house is being prepared for filming, Margaret Barry's reaction is one of

    A shock.

    B dismay.

    C apprehension.

    D resentment.

A	
B	
C	
D	

9 How is Jonathan Humphrey involved in the filming?

    A He controls the scale of the operation.

    B He represents the company's interests.

    C He makes safety checks.

    D He suggests a fee for the location.

A	
B	
C	
D	

10 What problem does the location manager outline?

    A Suitable properties are difficult to find.

    B Owners can refuse to allow their property to be used.

    C The character of a location may alter before filming.

    D Children like to play when filming is taking place.

A	
B	
C	
D	

11 Location managers are inclined to

    A treat the householder with disrespect.

    B keep rather quiet about the disruption involved.

    C make unreasonable demands on the occupants of the house.

    D offer the householder compensation if inconvenience is considerable.

A	
B	
C	
D	

12 When filming in her house had finished, Margaret Barry

    A said she would not want to repeat the experience.

    B complained about the confusion that had been caused.

    C considered that the benefits outweighed the disadvantages.

    D recommended the experience as a way of making extra money.

A	
B	
C	
D	

PART THREE

You will hear a discussion about the advantages and disadvantages of shops being open on a Sunday. Look at the points for and against, which are listed below. For questions **13-25**, put a tick (✓) beside the statements which are mentioned in the discussion.

(When transferring your answers, put the tick or leave blank, as appropriate, on the answer sheet.)

For		**Against**	
more convenient for shoppers	**13**	people would have to work on a Sunday	**20**
more profit for shops	**14**	there could be a change in the traditional pattern of the weekend	**21**
more trade for manufacturers	**15**	religious character of an English Sunday would be destroyed	**22**
more jobs	**16**	small shops would suffer	**23**
shops would be less crowded during the week	**17**	shop assistants would have to work unsocial hours	**24**
people would have more freedom to do what they want on Sundays	**18**	people who use small shops would be affected	**25**
many people want shops to open on Sundays	**19**		

PART FOUR

You will hear part of a radio programme in which a psychiatrist interviews a famous TV personality. For questions **26-30**, indicate which of the alternatives **A, B, C** or **D** is the most appropriate response.

(When transferring your answers, write A, B, C or D on the answer sheet.)

26 What sort of person does the interviewer believe Luke Kane to be?

   A   antisocial

   B   contradictory

   C   impatient

   D   unpredictable

A	
B	
C	
D	

27 What made Luke so difficult to work with?

   A   He had a low opinion of himself.

   B   He was intolerant of other people's behaviour.

   C   He was aware of growing old.

   D   He had unreasonably high standards.

A	
B	
C	
D	

28 Luke feels that his relationship with his mother was

   A   stormy.

   B   close.

   C   unusual.

   D   affectionate.

A	
B	
C	
D	

29 Luke remembers his father as someone

   A   he was extremely fond of.

   B   he shared everything with.

   C   he felt very sorry for.

   D   he spent long hours talking to.

A	
B	
C	
D	

30 What prompted Luke to consult a psychiatrist?

   A   His emotional instability.

   B   His inexplicable illness.

   C   His terrible experiences at sea.

   D   His guilt about not loving his mother.

A	
B	
C	
D	

PAPER 5 SPEAKING TEST   (about 15 minutes)

You will be asked to take part in a conversation with a group of other students or with your teacher. The conversation will be based on one particular topic area or theme, for example education, problems in society, the arts.

Of course each Speaking Test will be different for each student or group of students, but a *typical* test is described below.

★ At the start of the Speaking Test you will be asked to talk about one of the photographs among the Exercises on pages 123–125 at the back of the book; more than simple descriptions will be required.

★ You will then be asked to discuss one of the passages at the back of the book. Your teacher may ask you to talk about its content, where you think it comes from, who the author or speaker is, whether you agree or disagree with it, and so on. You will *not* be asked to read the passage aloud, but you may quote parts of it to make your point.

★ You may then be asked to discuss, for example, an advertisement, a leaflet, an extract from a newspaper, a quotation, etc. Your teacher will tell you which of the Speaking Test Exercises to look at.

★ You may also be asked to take part in an activity with a group of other students or your teacher which is intended to test your ability to interact successfully with other speakers during conversation and discussion in English. Your teacher will tell you which section among the Speaking Test Exercises you should look at.

Practice Test 5

PAPER 1 READING COMPREHENSION (1 hour)

There are **forty** questions on this paper. Attempt **all** questions. For each question there are four possible answers labelled **A, B, C** and **D**. Choose the **one** you consider correct and record your choice in **soft pencil** on the separate answer sheet.

Section A

In this section you must choose the word or phrase which best completes each sentence. **On your answer sheet**, indicate the letter **A, B, C** or **D** against the number of each item 1 to 25 for the word or phrase you choose. Give **one answer only** to each question.

1 The size of the pop-star's personal fortune was the subject of much ....
   in the press.
   A doubt   **B** guessing   **C** speculation   **D** wonderment

2 The manager of the shop was .... she would not give me a refund.
   A adamant   **B** dedicated   **C** abusive   **D** intent

3 Make sure you .... the cards before we start the next game.
   A turn   **B** mix   **C** alternate   **D** shuffle

4 Jeremy's friends were fond of him .... because of his generosity.
   A at least   **B** still less   **C** even less   **D** not least

5 The thick fog .... out any possibility of our plane taking off before
   morning.
   A ruled   **B** struck   **C** stamped   **D** crossed

6 Lack of rain early in the season meant that the fields .... a poor crop.
   A yielded   **B** generated   **C** surrendered   **D** suffered

7 Looking down at the coral reef, we saw .... of tiny, multi-coloured fish.
   A swarms   **B** flocks   **C** teams   **D** shoals

8 The doctor was praised for her .... work with her patients.
   A groundless   **B** tireless   **C** bottomless   **D** restless

9 Jack was .... to the fact that he couldn't take his holiday in June.
   A accepted   **B** complied   **C** agreed   **D** resigned

10 When it comes to the ...., Alice always supports her friends.
   A point   **B** crunch   **C** crisis   **D** finale

11 The transport minister .... recent statistics to support the case for a reduction in the speed limit.
   A named   **B** quoted   **C** summoned   **D** claimed

12 The amount Sarah earned was .... on how much she sold.
   A related   **B** connected   **C** dependent   **D** secured

13 The plan received .... support although none of the committee spoke openly in its favour.
   A tacit   **B** mute   **C** silent   **D** quiet

14 The junior staff were .... from all aspects of decision making.
   A excluded   **B** limited   **C** confined   **D** restricted

15 When the funds finally ...., they had to abandon the scheme.
   A faded away   **B** clamped down   **C** petered out   **D** fobbed off

16 The party leader travelled the length and .... of the country in an attempt to spread his message.
   A width   **B** distance   **C** diameter   **D** breadth

17 During the riots, there were .... between local residents and the police.
   A sieges   **B** demonstrations   **C** rallies.   **D** clashes

18 Sally has an .... command of the Chinese language.
   A extreme   **B** utter   **C** outstanding   **D** intensive

19 I am .... aware of the need to obey the rules of the competition.
   A well   **B** far   **C** much   **D** greatly

20 Richard started the race well but ran out of .... in the later stages.
   A power   **B** steam   **C** force   **D** effort

21 The move to a different environment had brought about a significant ....
   in Mary's state of mind.
   A impact   **B** effect   **C** influence   **D** change

22 The area .... considerable benefit from the setting up of a new factory.
   A merited   **B** derived   **C** achieved   **D** earned

23 Although the new library service has been very successful, its future is
.... certain.

    A at any rate   **B** by no means   **C** by all means   **D** by any chance

24 The Press thought the football manager would be depressed by his dismissal
but he just ....

    A ran it down   **B** called it off   **C** turned it down   **D** laughed it off

25 This excellent photograph has been .... in many leading magazines
around the world.

    A featured   **B** displayed   **C** portrayed   **D** disseminated

Section B

In this section you will find after each of the passages a number of questions or
unfinished statements about the passage, each with four suggested answers or
ways of finishing. You must choose the one which you think fits best. **On your
answer sheet**, indicate the letter **A**, **B**, **C** or **D** against the number of each item **26**
to **40** for the answer you choose. Give **one answer only** to each question.

FIRST PASSAGE

It is amazing how many people still say, 'I never dream', for it is now decades
since it was established that everyone has over a thousand dreams a year,
however few of these nocturnal productions are remembered on waking.
Even the most confirmed 'non-dreamers' will remember dreams if woken up
systematically during the rapid eye movement (REM) periods. These are
periods of light sleep during which the eyeballs move rapidly back and forth
under the closed lids and the brain becomes highly activated, which happens
three or four times every night of normal sleep.

It is a very interesting question why some people remember dreams
regularly – perhaps several a night on occasion – while others remember
hardly any at all under normal conditions. In considering this, it is important to
bear in mind that the dream tends to be an elusive phenomenon for all of us.
We normally never recall a dream unless we awaken directly from it, and even
then it has a tendency to fade quickly into oblivion.

Given this general elusiveness of dreams, the basic factor that seems to
determine whether a person remembers them or not is the same as that
which determines all other memory, namely degree of interest. Dream
researchers have made a broad classification of people into 'recallers' – those
who remember at least one dream a month – and 'non-recallers', who
remember fewer than this. Tests have shown that cool, analytical people with
a very rational approach to their feelings tend to recall fewer dreams than
those whose attitude to life is open and flexible. Engineers generally recall

fewer dreams than artists. It is not surprising to discover that in Western society, women normally recall more dreams than men, since women are traditionally allowed an instinctive, feeling approach to life.

In modern urban-industrial culture, feelings and dreams tend to be treated as frivolities which must be firmly subordinated to the realities of life. We pay lip-service to the inner life of imagination as it expresses itself in the arts, but in practice relegate music, poetry, drama and painting to the level of spare-time activities, valued mainly for the extent to which they refresh us for a return to work. We discourage our children from paying much attention to anything that might detract from the serious business of studying for exams or making a living in the 'real' world of industry and commerce.

26 Many people are unaware that they dream because
   A their dreams fade very quickly.
   B they do not recall their dreams.
   C they sleep too heavily.
   D they wake up frequently.

27 During REM periods, people
   A dream less.
   B wake up more easily.
   C remember their dreams more clearly.
   D experience discomfort.

28 People who remember their dreams do so because they
   A find the content relevant.
   B are awakened suddenly.
   C have retentive memories.
   D are regular dreamers.

29 Those who recall their dreams tend to be
   A practical.
   B unrealistic.
   C disorganised.
   D imaginative.

30 The writer believes that, in Western society, dreams are considered to be
   A shameful.
   B beneficial.
   C unimportant.
   D artistic.

SECOND PASSAGE

I never want to go home and I put if off as long as I can. I always walk, whatever the weather. And when I have got rid of my restlessness and my tendency to brood, I let myself into the flat and I am in for the rest of the evening. I have something to eat and then I usually try to write. In that way I manage to get rid of the rest of the day.

I encounter resistance in myself of course. That is only natural. I am quite young and I am aware that this is a dull life. Sometimes it seems like a physical effort to sit down at my desk and pull out the notebook. Sometimes I find myself heaving a sigh when I read through what I have already written. Sometimes the effort of putting pen to paper is so great that I literally feel a pain in my head, as if all the furniture of my mind were being rearranged, as if it were being lined up, being got ready for delivery to the storehouse. And yet when I start to write, all this heaviness vanishes, and I feel charged with a kind of electricity, not unpleasant in itself, but leading, inevitably, to greater restlessness.

Fortunately, I am not a hysterical person. I am used to being on my own and sometimes I doubt whether I could endure a lot of excitement. I am famous for my control, which has seen me through many crises. By a supreme irony, my control is so great that these crises remain unknown to the rest of the world, and so I am thought to be unfeeling. If I ever suffer loneliness, it is because I have settled for the harsh destiny of dealing with these matters by myself.

Sometimes I wish it were different. Sometimes I find myself lying awake in bed, wondering if this is to be my lot, if this solitude is to last for the rest of my days. Such thoughts sweep me to the edge of panic. For I want more, and I even think that I deserve it. I am no beauty but I am quite pleasant-looking. I am in good health and have ample private means. I have few bad habits, apart from my sharp tongue. I have no religion, but I observe certain rules of conduct with considerable piety. I feel quite deeply, I think. If I am not very careful, I shall grow into the most awful old battle-axe.

That is why I write, and why I have to. When I feel swamped in my solitude and hidden by it, physically obscured by it, rendered invisible, in fact, writing is my way of piping up. Of reminding people that I am here. And when I have ordered my characters, plundered my store of images, removed from them all the sadness that I might feel in myself, then I can switch on that current that allows me to write so easily, once I get started, and to make people laugh. That, it seems, is what they like to do. And if I manage this well enough and beguile all the critics, they will fail to register my real message, which is a simple one. If my looks and my manner were of greater assistance to me, I could deliver this message in person. 'Look at me,' I would say, 'Look at me.' But since I am on my own in this matter, I must use subterfuge and guile, and with a bit of luck and good management this particular message will never be deciphered, and my reasons for delivering it in this manner remain obscure.

31 Why does the writer take her time going home?
    A She enjoys the walk.
    B It's her chance to get some fresh air.
    C It settles her down.
    D She is unhappy with her accommodation.

32 Before starting to write in the evening, the writer
    A feels excited.
    B is worried that her work is not good enough.
    C rearranges the furniture.
    D forces herself to do what is needed.

33 The writer's behaviour in a crisis causes her to be
    A rejected.
    B ridiculed.
    C pitied.
    D misinterpreted.

34 How does the writer regard her life?
    A She is frustrated by it.
    B She is completely resigned to it.
    C She enjoys her solitude.
    D She has no desire to change.

35 What does the writer find attractive about writing?
    A Playing with words makes her feel powerful.
    B She expects one day to impress the critics.
    C It is her way of asserting her identity.
    D Writing makes her feel like someone else.

THIRD PASSAGE

In most aspects of medieval life, the closed corporation prevailed. But compared to modern life, the medieval urban family was a very open unit: for it included, as part of the normal household, not only relatives by blood but a group of industrial workers as well as domestics whose relation was that of secondary members of the family. This held for all classes, for young men from the upper classes got their knowledge of the world by serving as waiting men in a noble family: what they observed and overheard at mealtime was part of their education. Apprentices lived as members of the master craftsman's family. If marriage was perhaps deferred longer for men than today, the advantages of home life were not entirely lacking, even for the bachelor.

The workshop was a family; likewise the merchant's counting house. The members ate together at the same table, worked in the same rooms, slept in the same or common hall, converted at night into dormitories, joined in the family prayers, participated in the common amusements.

The intimate unity of domesticity and labour dictated the major arrangements within the medieval dwelling-house itself. Houses were usually built in continuous rows around the perimeter of their gardens. Free-standing houses, unduly exposed to the elements, wasteful of the land on each side, harder to heat, were relatively scarce: even farmhouses would be part of a solid block that included the stables, barns and granaries. The materials for the houses came out of the local soil, and they varied with the region. Houses in the continuous row forming the closed perimeter of a block, with guarded access on the ground floor, served as a domestic wall: a genuine protection against felonious entry in troubled times.

The earliest houses would have small window openings, with shutters to keep out the weather; then later, permanent windows of oiled cloth, paper and eventually glass. In the fifteenth century, glass, hitherto so costly it was used only for public buildings, became more frequent, at first only in the upper part of the window. A typical sixteenth-century window would have been divided into three panels: the uppermost panel, fixed, would be of diamond-paned glass; the next two panels would have shutters that opened inwards; thus the amount of exposure to sunlight and air could be controlled, yet on inclement days, both sets of shutters could be closed, without altogether shutting out the light. On any consideration of hygiene and ventilation this type of window was superior to the all-glass window that succeeded it, since glass excludes the bactericidal ultra-violet rays.

36 The urban family unit described in the passage
  A consisted of people related by blood.
  B was made up of workers, servants and family members.
  C excluded domestics and craftsmen.
  D was composed of members of the same social class.

37 How did young noblemen receive their education?
  A They were taught in their own homes.
  B They received training in practical skills.
  C They were sent to other households.
  D They were educated with other young men.

38 According to the writer, why were there few free-standing houses?
  A Building land was expensive.
  B Such houses were costly to construct.
  C Such houses suffered the effects of bad weather.
  D There was no room left for a garden.

39 Where could you have expected to find glass used in the fourteenth century?
  A in small windows in private houses
  B in buildings designed for public use
  C forming one part of a window protection
  D behind protective shutters

40 In the writer's opinion, all-glass windows were not an improvement because they were less
  A healthy.
  B attractive.
  C economical.
  D hard-wearing.

PAPER 2 COMPOSITION   (2 hours)

Answer any **two** questions.
Your answers must follow exactly the instructions given.
Write your answers on the separate answer paper provided.
Write clearly in pen, not pencil. You may make alterations but make sure that your
work is **easy to read.** Write both question numbers clearly in the left-hand margin at
the beginning of your answers.

1   Briefly describe the way in which you were brought up and then how you would
     bring up your own children. (About 350 words)

2   'Travel should broaden the mind and lead to better understanding, but it often
     fails to do so.' Discuss. (About 350 words)

3   Write a short story beginning or ending with the words: *She took the framed
     photo from the drawer and, with a smile, placed it carefully on the desk.* (About
     350 words)

4   A new company is producing a visitor's information guide and, as the local
     tourist officer, you have been asked to write a report on two contrasting eating
     places which you would recommend. You should cover such points as location,
     atmosphere, quality of food and service. (About 300 words)

5   Based on your reading of **one** of these books, write on **one** of the following.
     (About 350 words)

     RUTH PRAWER JHABVALA: *Heat and Dust*
     'Olivia's experiences are far more interesting to the reader than the narrator's.'
     Discuss.

     TIMOTHY MO: *Sour Sweet*
     Describe and contrast Lily and Mui, showing how each character contributes to
     the novel.

     WILLIAM GOLDING: *Lord of the Flies*
     Describe the developing conflict between Ralph and Jack and discuss its
     consequences.

PAPER 3 USE OF ENGLISH (2 hours)

Section A

1 Fill each of the numbered blanks in the passage with **one** suitable word.

Handling the interview

The aim of the interview is to provide a case history of the candidate. It may
(1) .... a tall order to expect a candidate to tell you the
(2) .... of his or her life in **(3)** .... time, usually quite
short, which is available for the interview. **(4)** .... candidates are
convinced that there is a sympathetic listener, however, it is surprising
(5) .... communicative they can become.

Conducting an interview successfully **(6)** .... essentially on two
things. The first is the establishment of **(7)** .... relationship with
candidates which will encourage **(8)** .... to talk freely about
themselves. This **(9)** .... be done if interviewers use interviews as
an opportunity to show **(10)** .... busy and important people they
are. **(11)** .... can it be done by a series of set formulae
(12) .... putting the candidate at ease, **(13)** .... as
shaking hands or offering coffee.

The second task is **(14)** .... steer the candidate over the
ground to be **(15)** .... so that the essential facts appear as quickly
as possible and irrelevancies are cut down to a **(16)** .... Each
remark **(17)** .... guide the candidate to talk about the right things
(18) .... interrupting the flow of conversation. Each interview is

(19) .... and foremost a conversation, and **(20)** .... it is successful as such it will never be a good interview.

2   Finish each of the following sentences in such a way that it is **as similar as possible in meaning to the sentence printed before it.**

EXAMPLE: I expect that he will get there by lunchtime.

ANSWER: I expect him *to get there by lunchtime.*

a) It was to be another twenty-five years before Michael returned to his home town.

Not until ....

    ....

b) Melissa's father was very busy, but he still played with her.

Busy ....

    ....

c) Mrs Wilson says she's sorry she didn't attend the meeting yesterday morning.

Mrs Wilson sends ....

    ....

d) It's almost nine months since I stopped subscribing to that magazine.

I cancelled ....

    ....

e) For further information, please send a self-addressed envelope to the above address.

Further information can ....

    ....

f) Richard only took over the family business because his father decided to retire early.

But for his ....

    ....

g) It shouldn't have surprised me that my children didn't like the new, cheaper ice-cream.

I might ....

....

h) The northwest of Britain has more rain each year than the southeast.

The annual ....

....

3 Fill each of the blanks with a suitable word or phrase.

EXAMPLE: He doesn't mind one way or the other; it makes *no difference to* him.

a) Had the lecturer realised that people couldn't hear her, she

.... louder.

b) Those books you bought were .... money. You've never even opened them.

c) I've got to give an after-dinner speech next week and I can't think of

.... say.

d) Put all the toys away .... someone slips and falls on them.

e) It's .... question for the children to watch the late-night film.

f) If they don't have a telephone, there's no way we .... know that the concert has been cancelled.

4 For each of the sentences below, write a new sentence **as similar as possible in meaning to the original sentence**, but using the word given. This word **must not be altered in any way.**

EXAMPLE: Not many people attended the meeting.
    turnout

ANSWER: *There was a poor turnout for the meeting.*

a) You won't solve your problems by getting a bank loan.
solution

....

....

b) The impression most people have of him is that he is an honest person.
comes

....

....

c) The new plans for the school have been approved by the authorities.
met

....

....

d) Fred has only himself to blame for losing his driving licence for repeated speeding.
serves

....

....

e) By being absent so often Jim failed the examination.
cost

....

....

f) The severity of the punishment bore no relation to the seriousness of the crime.
proportion

....

....

g) I'm sure the entertainer will cheer them all up.
bound

....

....

h) Don't forget those who are at work on this lovely, sunny day!
spare

....

....

Section B

5   Read this passage, then answer the questions which follow it.

The Art business

Whilst it is wonderful to have the time to concentrate entirely on painting, those wishing to 'go it alone' will need far more than creative flair to succeed independently. Being a professional artist is a business which, like all others, will only flourish if there is a steady demand for the particular skills and products offered and if the business structure and 5 finances are sound. Some optimism is essential, of course, though this won't keep you solvent! For some perhaps that wealthy patron will appear, but for most it will pay to be realistic and astute about business funding.

It is important to have a long-term strategy, a business plan, and 10 adequate initial cash, if your business is to get off the ground and begin to develop. Preparing yourself with the right equipment and materials, setting up a studio, building up contacts, advertising and so on will make a heavy demand on basic capital. Add to this the fact that there is often quite a long delay between the completion of work and the actual 15 payment and you can see that certainly the first year of business is not going to be very profitable. Obviously, initial investment has to be sensibly weighed against likely sales. For example, a printmaker who has secured a few lucrative contracts can safely borrow capital to purchase a new press; perhaps likewise a potter investing in a kiln. 20

However, purchasing such equipment and materials is very often more of a calculated gamble. Take, for instance, the painter who spends a large sum on framing work for an exhibition for which there are no guaranteed sales. Artists are frequently paid on completion of a commission, have work on sale-or-return or are paid royalties or fees well 25 after the work has been finished. So cash flow can be a problem.

I recently heard that there are something like 50,000 independent artists and craftspeople in the UK, of whom only about fifty are running a commercially viable business. Whilst I cannot verify these figures and whilst definitions of 'an artist' and 'a commercially viable business' are 30 debatable, the comment does rather drive home the difficulties that face the would-be professional. I do not intend to paint a picture of all doom and gloom: indeed, I would encourage those with serious intentions of turning professional. But, writing as a freelance artist who, amongst many, has been through hard times, I should be irresponsible if I failed to point 35 out the real problems we face.

So, start with some clear aims and targets. You will need to make a business plan which ideally covers the first two or three years. Give this careful thought, and cost likely expenses realistically. Make a professional

job of the preparation of such a plan – you may well find that you need 40
copies of it to support applications for grants, loans and sponsorship. Any
assumptions about probable income should be kept on the conservative
side, and don't proceed with the venture if it looks financially too risky.

Because of the unpredictable nature of business, many artists are
naturally wary of borrowing money. Instead, they are prepared to 45
compromise in their quest to 'do their own thing' and supplement their
income through part-time work or by diversifying into other aspects and
markets related to their particular discipline and form of work.

It is a question of striking the right balance: whilst there are
advantages in working elsewhere and maintaining various contacts with 50
the outside world, these must not demand so much that it becomes
impossible to meet commission deadlines or maintain and develop studio
work as you would like.

Few artists make the sort of income they could attract in public
service or a commercial organisation. It is a sad reflection on society in 55
general that the work of artists is not better recognised, appreciated and
rewarded. However, it is a path we choose to tread in the knowledge that
the gains will be other than material! Nevertheless, it is as well to have a
determined financial strategy which has been realistically planned.

a) Which word earlier in the first paragraph does the phrase 'realistic and
astute' (line 8) contrast with?

....

....

b) What is meant by the phrase 'building up contacts' in line 13?

....

....

c) Explain in your own words when it would be sensible for a printmaker to
borrow money to buy a new press.

....

....

d) Explain in your own words the writer's view of an artist spending large
amounts of money on framing work.

....

....

e) Why is the writer sceptical about the figures quoted in the fourth paragraph?

....

....

f) What effect does the writer fear these figures might have on the 'would-be professional'? (line 32)

....

....

g) What **two** considerations should influence the figures in an artist's business plan?

....

....

h) How might taking a part-time job represent a compromise for an artist?

....

....

i) What is the 'balance' referred to in line 49?

....

....

j) What phrase in the last paragraph underlines the writer's criticism of the way artists are treated?

....

....

k) What is meant in this context by the phrase 'other than material'? (line 58)

....

....

l) What is the function of this article?

....

....

m) In a paragraph of 70-90 words, summarise the financial difficulties which, in the opinion of the author, are faced by those who decide to become professional artists.

....

....

....

....

....

....

....

....

....

....

....

....

....

....

PAPER 4 LISTENING COMPREHENSION (about 35 minutes)

In the live examination, you will have to transfer your answers to the separate answer sheet. See page 134 for a sample answer sheet.

PART ONE

You will hear a conversation between a man and woman about their nephew, Matthew. For questions **1-9**, indicate the correct response by circling TRUE or FALSE.

(When transferring your answers, write T or F on the answer sheet.)

1	Matthew helps with the housework.	TRUE/FALSE
2	The parents refuse to pay college fees.	TRUE/FALSE
3	Matthew has saved up a lot of money.	TRUE/FALSE
4	The uncle dislikes travelling abroad.	TRUE/FALSE
5	Matthew did well in his exams.	TRUE/FALSE
6	Matthew has refused an interesting job.	TRUE/FALSE
7	The parents have given Matthew a deadline for his decision.	TRUE/FALSE
8	The aunt believes the uncle is too severe.	TRUE/FALSE
9	The uncle accepts that Matthew needs some more time to decide.	TRUE/FALSE

PART TWO

You will hear a woman, Mrs Norton, being interviewed for a job. For questions **10-19**, complete the interviewer's notes with a few words.

(When transferring your answers, write the word or short phrase, as appropriate, on the answer sheet.)

<u>Past five years:</u>

Year 1	10
Year 2	11
Year 3	12
Year 4	13
Year 5	14

<u>Reasons for wanting THIS job:</u>

similar [15] to Softlight

chance to start [16]

has heard about our [17]

<u>Her questions</u>

structure of our [18]

childcare for [19]

PART THREE

You will hear part of a radio programme. In it Dr Menzies describes working in Antarctica. For questions **20-25**, indicate which of the alternatives **A, B, C** or **D** is the most appropriate response.

(When transferring your answers, write A, B, C or D on the answer sheet.)

20 Why has Dr Menzies been chosen to appear on the programme?

    A because she does a job normally done by men

    B because she works in the Antarctic

    C because she does research into the ozone layer

    D because she works abroad

A	
B	
C	
D	

21 What does she do on arriving at Rothera?

    A She starts her research work.

    B She prepares her plane.

    C She rests before continuing her journey.

    D She gets ready for work in the field.

A	
B	
C	
D	

22 How did the men react to her at first?

    A They were rude to her.

    B They tried to protect her.

    C They disapproved of her presence.

    D They tried to impress her.

A	
B	
C	
D	

23 How does she feel about the dogs at the base?

    A She regards them as her friends.

    B She wishes she could take them home with her.

    C She believes they should not be treated like pets.

    D She relies on them for her safety.

A	
B	
C	
D	

24 What does she consider the best aspect of her work?

    A   riding on a sledge

    B   the beginning of each expedition

    C   the place itself

    D   living in a tent

A	
B	
C	
D	

25 What does she describe as 'extraordinary'?

    A   the size of the glaciers

    B   the combination of colours

    C   the whiteness everywhere

    D   the red of the vehicles

A	
B	
C	
D	

PAPER 5 SPEAKING TEST   (about 15 minutes)

You will be asked to take part in a conversation with a group of other students or with your teacher. The conversation will be based on one particular topic area or theme, for example education, problems in society, the arts.

Of course each Speaking Test will be different for each student or group of students, but a *typical* test is described below.

★ At the start of the Speaking Test you will be asked to talk about one of the photographs among the Exercises on pages 126–128 at the back of the book; more than simple descriptions will be required.

★ You will then be asked to discuss one of the passages at the back of the book. Your teacher may ask you to talk about its content, where you think it comes from, who the author or speaker is, whether you agree or disagree with it, and so on. You will *not* be asked to read the passage aloud, but you may quote parts of it to make your point.

★ You may then be asked to discuss, for example, an advertisement, a leaflet, an extract from a newspaper, a quotation, etc. Your teacher will tell you which of the Speaking Test Exercises to look at.

★ You may also be asked to take part in an activity with a group of other students or your teacher which is intended to test your ability to interact successfully with other speakers during conversation and discussion in English. Your teacher will tell you which section among the Speaking Test Exercises you should look at.

Speaking Test Exercises

PRACTICE TEST 1

HELP

1

2

3

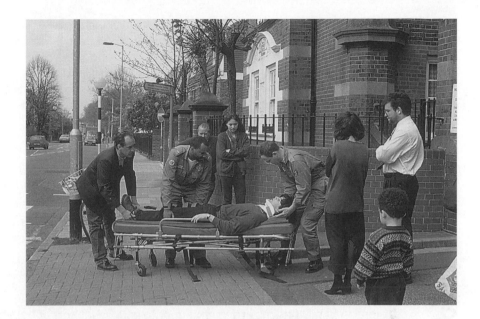

4

> ## Artificial Respiration
>
> Needed when the patient has stopped breathing for himself.
> In this emergency NO TIME CAN BE WASTED.
> Resuscitation must begin AT ONCE with no moments spared to
> place the patient's (or rescuer's) body comfortably. A drowned
> person, for instance, must receive artificial respiration as soon
> as his head is free from water.
>
> **DELAY OF ONE OR TWO SECONDS MAY PROVE FATAL**

5

Superstitious practices appear in every epoch and every culture. They
are numerous and varied and are almost all totally meaningless and
futile except in one basic respect; namely, that they make the
performers of the actions feel a little safer in a hostile and mysterious
world. They all consist of some activity which, if performed, is
supposed to prevent bad luck in the future. The fact that there is
never any logical connection between the act and the outcome does
nothing to deter the superstitious.

6   Who are the displaced people and refugees? Why are they in camps? What are their problems and needs? How are their lives affected by the current conflict? What is their future? Who gains from their plight? Why are the United Nations, the International Red Cross, and other humanitarian agencies unable to fulfil their mandates of protection? Why have so few diplomatic efforts been made to end the suffering? These are but a few of the questions involved in an understanding of the border situation.

7   *'I don't know what I would have done without the help of my friends.'*

'I never ask anyone for help. In the end, you can only rely on yourself.'

8   A foreign family has moved in next door to you. What sort of help might they need? What could you offer them?

9

Technological Aids

- air conditioning/central heating
- calculator
- camera
- car
- computer
- cooker
- glasses (= spectacles)
- photocopier
- telephone
- watch

PRACTICE TEST 2

HEROES

1

2

3

4

According to the latest figures from the National School
Safety Center, an estimated 135,000 children carry a gun to
school every day in the USA. Another 270,000 take a gun to
school at least once. Last year Andre Easley, aged fifteen,
was expelled from his Detroit school for carrying a gun.
'I got into an argument with a boy and his friends over
something stupid during the holidays. So when we went back
to school, I got a gun from a friend to take with me.'

5

In 1980 Reinhold Messner risked 'madness' as some called it: the ascent
of the north face of Mount Everest.

Completely alone during the adverse weather conditions of the
monsoon season, Messner climbed for days at altitudes known to
mountaineers as the death zone. Without oxygen equipment; without a
partner; without the possibility of rescue.

But one piece of equipment Messner never climbs without is his Rolex
Oyster quartz.

'To be up there without a precise and absolutely reliable watch would
be madness,' says Messner.

6

THE DANCE MASTER

Rudolph Nureyev bestrode the ballet world like a colossus. One of the
greatest dancers of this century, he was also among the most legendary
figures in any branch of the theatre of our time. His spectacular arrival in
the West in the early 1960s gave a huge boost to the appeal of classical
dance, and – by his blend of technical brilliance, expressive artistry and
charismatic stage presence – he transformed our image of the male dancer.

7

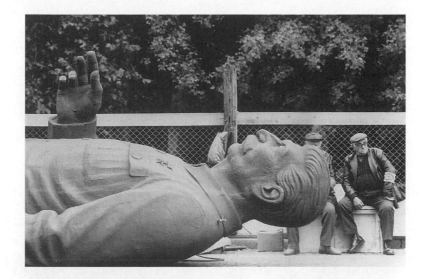

8

EXTERMINATOR

⑮

NO ONE IS SAFE

X

SQUAD

⑮

9

"Some are born great, some achieve greatness and some have greatness thrust upon them."

(William Shakespeare, *Twelfth Night*)

PRACTICE TEST 3

THE GOOD LIFE

1

2

3

4

ISLAND OF TRANQUILLITY
Guernsey. Where secluded bays and safe, sandy beaches, winding country lanes and stunning clifftop views can all be discovered and explored at an unhurried pace.

Guernsey is peaceful, quiet, relaxing, restful and it has beautiful scenery. Each word says something about this enchanting holiday island. And yet one word says it all. Tranquillity.

5

I was the only child of my mother and father and had always felt I would return one day to the house my father built. Now I've just had a birthday lunch there, with eighteen children and grand-children. It's nice to see them playing in the same woods I played in and doing the same things I did. My young daughter is already attached to the place. She's seven, and goes to the village school, and lives with animals (ponies and dogs) and friends. I don't think she would have any happiness suddenly being wrenched away to foreign parts.

6   **Quality of life**
    The new 16 valve, 1.6 Hyundai Lantra
    Why condemn yourself to a featureless existence when you could
    live life to the full in the brilliant new Hyundai Lantra?
    Not just another new car, but a new concept that offers new values
    in motoring with levels of performance, ride, handling, comfort and
    equipment that put it in a class of its own.

7

Problems of the 1990s

- hunger
- homelessness/lack of shelter
- disease
- unemployment
- inflation
- family break-ups e.g. separation, divorce
- poverty
- political/religious intolerance

8

'The Good Life'

- luxurious accommodation
- servants
- antique furniture and furnishings
- expensive clothes and jewellery
- luxury cars
- a private aeroplane or yacht
- a life of leisure
- parties and entertainment
- exotic holidays

9

'I know what things are good: friendship and work and conversation.'

'If you don't have money, you can't enjoy the good things in life.'

PRACTICE TEST 4

PROGRESS

1

2

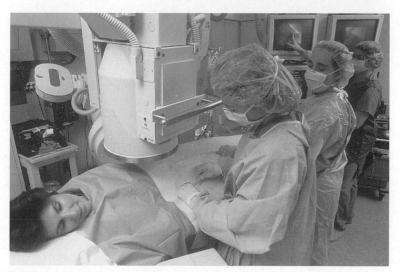

3

4 In the sixteen years or so since development first came to this country, I have watched the gap between rich and poor widen; I have watched women lose their self-confidence and power; I have watched the appearance of unemployment and inflation and a dramatic rise in crime; I have watched population levels soar, fuelled by a variety of economic and psychological pressures; I have watched the disintegration of families and communities; and I have watched people become separated from the land, as self-sufficiency is gradually replaced by economic dependence on the outside world.

5 Traffic in central London is travelling at its slowest rate since record-keeping began, according to the latest Department of Transport figures. The average day-time traffic speed in central London is 10.2 m.p.h. Klaus Meyer, of the campaign group Transport 2000, said: 'We're back to the speed of the horse and carriage and things are just going to get worse until action is taken to get cars off the roads.'

6 Charlotte Hughes was born on August 2nd, 1887, the day Alexander Graham Bell launched his first telephone company. She has travelled by horse-drawn carriage and Concorde, seen the birth of the record player, the fax machine and the first test tube baby. Her memories, which she recalls vividly even now, are part of our history books. 'Life is not better now,' she says. 'It's different.'

7

'What we call progress is the exchange of one nuisance for another nuisance.'

'Without progress we are nothing: progress is the essence of man's life on earth.'

8

Inventions and Discoveries

- the wheel
- the internal combustion engine
- the postal service
- the electric light bulb
- the printing press
- the microchip
- penicillin

9

Progress

- public transport
- housing
- education
- health
- standards of living
- the economy

PRACTICE TEST 5

STRANGE THINGS

1

2

3

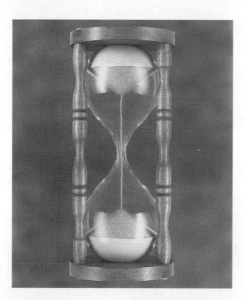

4 Ghosts, dreams, second sight, precognition, these are only a few of the mysterious worlds explored in this remarkable and well-documented book. The author deals with matters that have perplexed, terrified or fascinated mankind since the beginning of recorded history, including foreknowledge, going back in time, divination, witchcraft and telepathy. It is bound to become one of the most memorable books of the year.

5 In and around the area known as the 'Bermuda Triangle' many ships, planes and small boats have reportedly disappeared under mysterious circumstances. The reports of these disappearances quickly eliminated possible logical causes and attributed the losses to strange, unknown forces. However, the main causes are precisely what the creators of the legend said were not at fault: bad weather, human error and mechanical failure. The Bermuda Triangle mystery is a manufacture perpetuated by careless research and sensational reporting.

6 The most celebrated example of clairvoyance ('seeing' things that are happening a long way away) was that by Emmanuel Swedenborg, on 19 July 1759. He described in vivid detail to a meeting of local officials in Göteborg, the progress of a disastrous fire which was sweeping through Stockholm, 300 miles away. At six he told them the fire had just broken out; at eight he told them it had been extinguished only three doors from his home. Two days later a messenger from Stockholm confirmed every detail.

7

Life on Other Planets
We have proof, scientist claims

Piano-playing ghost
Eighteenth century lady plays for children while parents sleep

'I know I've been here before.'

Film star describes previous lives in ancient Egypt and medieval London

8

Good luck or bad luck?

9

Madame Celeste
Tell me your dreams and I will help you:
understand your past,
control your present,
influence your future.
For a personal consultation phone 0181 237 8954

OPTIONAL READING

Timothy Mo: *Sour Sweet*

1

2

翠 亨 邨 酒 家

London Chinatown Restaurant Ltd.
27 Gerrard Street, London W1
Tel: 071-437-3186

3

4

5

6

NB The page numbers given after the extracts refer to the Abacus edition of the book.

7   Only with difficulty would Lily persuade her to come to the sitting-room, when she deposited Mui on the sibilant black sofa and tried to draw her out. It wasn't easy to find out what was wrong with Mui. Mui herself didn't seem to know. She had worked for a foreigner before. Perhaps it was the concentration of them here she found so disturbing. (*page 9*)

8   Her father made no concessions to his pupil. He had the child squatting in a low crouch for an hour at a time with legs apart as far as they could stretch, using two daggers stuck in the ground as markers. On her head he balanced a full earthenware wine-jar of the smaller type (a hard man, he was also a realist). At the same time he lightly rapped Lily's shins with a bamboo staff. (*page 11*)

9   Grass Sandal took a deep breath. She had weighed out on tiny, apothecary's scales 115 grams of the crude brown No 3 mixture stored under a floor board and placed it on a thick block of glass. To this she added ten grams of a base powder. She mixed it with the pyramid of No 3. The result was not entirely satisfactory from the point of view of texture. (*page 54*)

10   Chen considered stopping. This was a good start anyway. He might be able to do something with this to get more cash. Roman again seemed to have a window into his thoughts. 'Bad to stop now, Uncle. Follow luck through. You are a lucky man tonight.' Chen reluctantly put down another stake. Won. Yet again he won. He now won for the fourth time in succession. Perhaps he could win the entire sum tonight, perhaps in the next ten minutes! (*page 63*)

11   Superstition also encouraged the girls to fall in with Chen's plans. In Chinese Street Lily had bought a wonderful household god; red-skinned, pot bellied, with a fearsome scowl and curling black mustachios, nine squatting inches of concentrated energy which lit up with a baleful glow when the bulb in its interior was wired to the mains. (*page 92*)

12 The food they sold, certainly wholesome, nutritious, colourful, even tasty in its way, had been researched by Chen. It bore no resemblance at all to Chinese cuisine. They served from a stereotyped menu, similar to those outside countless other establishments in the UK. The food was, if nothing else, thought Lily, provenly successful: English tastebuds must be as degraded as their care of their parents; it could, of course, be part of a scheme of cosmic repercussion. (*page 105*)

13 'How handsome Son has grown! How tall, how big!' Mrs Law was genuinely pleased and surprised at the transformation in Man Kee after six months.
   'Yes, Big Head.'
   Lily darted a furious look at Husband. Traitorous, flippant Husband. She gathered Man Kee in her arms and kissed the top of his head, which was no longer downy but a thick poll. 'He has a beautiful head. Nothing wrong with its proportions.' (*page 125*)

14 Iron Plank moved in fast, describing a shuffling in-and-out circular movement with his feet, twirling the pair of short swords so that they resembled the wings of a butterfly. Jackie swung his axe clumsily and Iron Plank trapped it with both blades. But the telegraphed blow was a feint. Iron Plank found himself sprawled on the carpet from a neat ankle-tap. (*page 133*)

15 Next Chen had trouble with the steering. The van crept slowly towards the white lines on the middle of the road, then over into the other lane. As Chen desperately over-compensated, the van veered back over the camber and down onto the pavement, straight for the gate where the spectators were standing. Lily and Mui had as their first inclinations a healthy desire to retreat down the steps, instantly suppressed in the interests of preserving Chen's face. (*page 149*)

16 'Now Mar-Mar teaches how to give kick.' She showed him the cardinal kicks up to the waist, using the heel and edge of the foot (toe and instep were too fragile for a child's foot or untrained man's in a cloth shoe). The strikes were to shin, knee-cap and groin. 'Clever boy!' This wasn't encouragement. Lily really meant it. Man Kee was a natural, a real natural, with his feet. (*page 232*)

17 Grandpa stepped forward. With as much of a flourish as his arthritic shoulder permitted him, he whipped off the tarpaulin. Lily blinked. She knew the shape of what she was looking at; it took just a moment to absorb and digest its significance. Propped against the wall at a 45 degree angle were a coffin and coffin-lid in smooth but unvarnished wood. (*page 253*)

18 As if to make up to Husband for her negligence in bringing his son up properly, the way she was sure he in his heart of hearts would want him brought up (never mind what he seemed to want on the surface), she repeatedly dinned into Son the example of his father. Overnight, Chen had become a secular saint, a household deity to rival god. (*page 274*)

DISCUSSION TOPICS

19 *Sour Sweet* was filmed recently. If you have seen the film, what did you think of it? Did it portray the characters as you imagined them?

20 'The workings of Husband's mind could be mysterious. One pulled levers and hoped the right combination would click somewhere in there.' How much do you think Chen and Lily understand each other? Discuss their relationship.

21 What do you learn about Chinese family life, traditions and values from the book?

22 What are the main features of the Wo Society? Describe its organisation. How much do you blame Chen for getting involved with it?

23 What do you think happens to Lily and Mui after the ending of the book?

24 Do you think Man Kee grows up as rooted in Chinese traditions as his family? Why (not)?

CAMBRIDGE
EXAMINATIONS, CERTIFICATES & DIPLOMAS
ENGLISH AS A FOREIGN LANGUAGE

University of Cambridge
Local Examinations Syndicate
International Examinations

FOR SUPERVISOR'S USE ONLY
Shade here if the candidate
is ABSENT or has WITHDRAWN

↳ ▭

X

Examination/Paper No.	9999/01
Examination Title	FCE or CPE EXAM
Centre/Candidate No.	AA999/9999
Candidate Name	A.N. EXAMPLE

99/D99

● Sign here if the information above is correct

● Tell the Invigilator immediately if the information above
is not correct.

M U L T I P L E – C H O I C E   A N S W E R   S H E E T

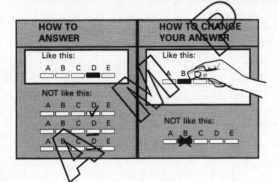

DO
- use an HB pencil
- rub out any answer
  you wish to change

DON'T
- use any other kind of pen
  or pencil
- use correcting fluid
- make any marks outside
  the boxes

1	A B C D
2	A B C D
3	A B C D
4	A B C D
5	A B C D
6	A B C D
7	A B C D
8	A B C D
9	A B C D
10	A B C D

11	A B C D
12	A B C D
13	A B C D
14	A B C D
15	A B C D
16	A B C D
17	A B C D
18	A B C D
19	A B C D
20	A B C D

21	A B C D
22	A B C D
23	A B C D
24	A B C D
25	A B C D
26	A B C D
27	A B C D
28	A B C D
29	A B C D
30	A B C D

31	A B C D
32	A B C D
33	A B C D
34	A B C D
35	A B C D
36	A B C D
37	A B C D
38	A B C D
39	A B C D
40	A B C D

Sample Answer Sheets

 University of Cambridge
Local Examinations Syndicate
International Examinations

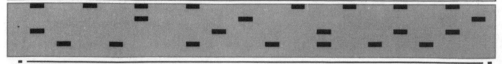

| FOR SUPERVISOR'S USE ONLY |
| Shade here if the candidate |
| is ABSENT or has WITHDRAWN |

Examination/Paper No.   9999/04   99/D99

Examination Title   ANY CAMBRIDGE EXAM

Centre/Candidate No.   AA999/9999

Candidate Name   A.N. EXAMPLE

● Sign here if the information above is correct.

● Tell the Invigilator immediately if the
  information above is not correct.

LISTENING COMPREHENSION ANSWER SHEET

ENTER TEST NUMBER HERE →

FOR OFFICE USE ONLY →   FCE CAE CPE [00][10][20][30][40][50][60][70][80][90]
                          [1][5][3]   [0][1][2][3][4][5][6][7][8][9]

1		1	21		21
2		2	22		22
3		3	23		23
4		4	24		24
5		5	25		25
6		6	26		26
7		7	27		27
8		8	28		28
9		9	29		29
10		10	30		30
11		11	31		31
12		12	32		32
13		13	33		33
14		14	34		34
15		15	35		35
16		16	36		36
17		17	37		37
18		18	38		38
19		19	39		39
20		20	40		40

EFL-4   KENRICK JEFFERSON   Printers to the Computer Industry   DP150/31

You may photocopy this page.   © **UCLES/K&J**